NAPOLEON
and the Awakening of Europe

NAPOLEON
and
the Awakening of Europe

FELIX MARKHAM

Fellow of
Hertford College, Oxford

THE ENGLISH UNIVERSITIES PRESS LTD

ISBN O 340 08366 2

First published 1954
Eighth impression 1972

The English Universities Press Ltd
St Paul's House, Warwick Lane, London EC4P 4AH

Printed in Great Britain by
Biddles Ltd, Guildford, Surrey

Introduction to the Series

This series has been undertaken in the conviction that no subject is more important than history. For though the conquests of natural science (nuclear fission, the exploration of space, genetic advance, bacteriology, etc.) have given their character to the age, it is actually a greater need to gain control of the forces of nature loosed upon us. The prime urgency, the deepest necessity is in the human field: to understand the nature and condition of man as a pre-condition of better controls, and fewer disasters, in the world of politics and society.

There is no better introduction to this sphere, and the understanding of its problems, than history. *Some* knowledge of history, we feel, ought to prevent some mistakes: at every point we can learn vicariously from the experience of others before us.

To take one point only—the understanding of politics: how can we understand the world of affairs around us, if we do not know how it came to be what it is? How to interpret the United States, or Soviet Russia, France, Germany or Britain without some knowledge of their history?

Some evidence of the growing awareness of this may be seen in the great increase of interest in history among the general public, and in the much larger place the subject has come to take in education.

The most congenial, as well as the most concrete and practical, approach to history is the biographical: through the lives of great men whose careers have been significant in history. Fashions in historical writing have their ups and downs; men's and women's lives have their perennial interest—though in this series we are chiefly concerned to show their historical significance, the contribution they made to their age: *Men and their Times*.

A generation ago historical biographies were rather unfashionable with analytical historians and technicians, like· Namier: he ended by writing scores of miniature biographies of M.P.s. The detailed analysis of Civil War and Commonwealth has ended by showing that there were almost as many party-divisions as there were individuals. We are back in the realm of biography and the biographical approach to history, since there is no greater diversity, variety and subtlety than in the lives of individual men and women, particularly those who left a mark on their time.

A. L. Rowse
Oxford

Contents

Chapter One

The Young Corsican

"I HAVE a presentiment that one day this small island will astonish Europe." So Rousseau wrote of Corsica in his *Contrat Social*, which appeared in 1762, seven years before the birth of Napoleon Buonaparte at Ajaccio (August 15, 1769). Rousseau was thinking of a small, proud and brave people who were fighting successfully for their independence under their patriot leader, Paoli, against the Genoese. When the French secured by treaty the Genoese rights over Corsica and invaded the island in 1769, Paoli was defeated and went into exile in England.

Carlo Buonaparte, the father of Napoleon, was one of Paoli's closest supporters and protégés, but he quickly made his peace with the French and rose to a prominent position in the new French administration. He was a handsome, polished and extravagant man, adept at pulling political strings. His wife, Letizia Ramolino, daughter of a government official of Genoese origin, was cast in the mould of a Roman matron. Mother of eight Buonapartes—Joseph, Napoleon, Lucien, Elisa, Louis, Pauline, Caroline and Jérôme—she had classic beauty but little education. She was brave, hardy and fiercely maternal, but stern and economical in the management of her household. In later years her parsimony became a Parisian joke. "Provided it lasts," she would say. "She must save against the day when she might have seven or eight kings on her hands."

It was the influence of his friend de Marbœuf, the

French governor of Corsica, that enabled Carlo Buonaparte to secure the nomination to a scholarship in the
College of Autun for his elder son, Joseph, and to the
Military Academy at Brienne for his second son, Napoleon. Brienne was one of twelve royal military schools
founded and organised by the Minister of War in 1776
for the sons of nobles, and entry to it required strict evidence of noble descent as well as influential recommenda-
tions. Carlo Buonaparte was able to produce proof of
noble lineage at least since the sixteenth century, when
his branch of the Buonaparte family left the Genoese
mainland to settle in Corsica.

Great men have seldom been happy or successful
schoolboys; but the hardships and unpopularity of Napoleon at school have been exaggerated, partly by his recol-
lections in the memoirs, partly by later forgeries of letters
and school reports. It appears from the evidence that
Napoleon was an outstanding scholar in mathematics and
passionately interested in history; that he was of a romantic, melancholy and self-willed temperament, somewhat
solitary but capable of acquiring a few close friends. One
of the more amiable traits in his character which he retained as Emperor was—and like his sense of family
loyalty, it was a typically Corsican characteristic—his
remembrance of the friends and teachers of his youth.
Nearly all of them benefited by pensions and places. His
old nurse was present at his coronation and introduced
at court. A few but by no means all of his masters discovered the hidden depths in his character. He was
always old for his years, and his sense of responsibility
was increased by the early death of his father in 1785,
leaving him, as a much stronger character than Joseph,
the effective head of the family.

Napoleon appeared as somewhat of an oddity to his
school-fellows, since he clung passionately to the idea that

he was an alien patriot among his French conquerors. His heroes were Paoli and Rousseau, the champion of Roman virtue and of oppressed small nations. He was, therefore, mildly but not excessively ragged at Autun (where he went first at the age of nine and a half for three months before proceeding to Brienne), and, from the sound of his name, nicknamed 'Straw-nose' ('Paille-au-nez-Napollione'). His first ambition was to enter the navy, but at the end of his time at Brienne he was selected for the army cadet school at Paris. This was a smart, aristocratic and even luxurious establishment, but hard-working. Napoleon's distinction in mathematics was such that, at his leaving examination for the artillery corps, he was placed forty-second on the whole national list by Laplace, the famous mathematician, and was commissioned as a lieutenant, jumping the intermediate grades of probationer and pupil.

At the end of 1785, he was posted to the Régiment de la Fère, stationed at Valence in the Rhône valley. At St. Helena he recalled his first flirtation, at Valence, with a girl called Caroline de Colombier. "It will scarcely be considered credible, perhaps, but our whole business consisted in eating cherries together." In later years he continued to correspond with this girl after her marriage, and paid a visit to her in 1805 as Emperor. (To the embarrassment of the poor lady, her butler upset the soup-tureen over the Emperor.) For the aristocratic officer of the *ancien régime* prolonged leave was absurdly easy to obtain, and between 1786 and 1788, when he was posted to Auxonne, he was able to spend three-quarters of his time in Corsica or Paris. It was the first time he had returned to his family since he had left for school eight years before.

The events of 1789 were greeted by Napoleon with enthusiasm, steeped as he was in the ideas of the Enlighten-

3

ment; though his first contact with these events was limited to the suppression of minor food riots in the neighbourhood of Auxonne. The rank and file of his regiment and the majority of his brother officers were sympathetic to the Revolution; and this was typical of the whole artillery corps. Whereas the officers of the line regiments emigrated *en masse*, particularly after 1791, in a sort of general strike against the Revolution, the artillery officers, better educated and drawn mainly from the minor, poor *noblesse*, were more inclined to stay in their posts. (One of Napoleon's fellow cadets, Phélipeaux, who emigrated, commanded Sidney Smith's guns which halted Napoleon at Acre in 1799.) The artillery corps was thus able to retain its discipline and cohesion, and it was probably this fact that saved the Revolution in 1792 in the artillery duel of Valmy.

Napoleon saw in the Revolution primarily an opportunity of freedom for Corsica; his thoughts were still dominated by Corsica and Rousseau. He was planning to write a history of Corsica, and drafted a memorandum to be sent to Necker (*Lettres sur la Corse*). As late as 1791, the discourse he wrote for a prize offered by the Academy of Lyons is pure Rousseau. The argument is in almost ludicrous contrast to his later sense of values. The ambition of Alexander is severely condemned. Later, he was to say of Rousseau : "He was a madman who has brought us to the state we are in now."

In September 1789, Napoleon returned to Corsica on leave, and plunged into local politics on the radical side, helping to form a national citizen guard in defiance of the authorities. In November 1789, the Constituent Assembly at Paris decreed the incorporation of Corsica into France, extending to Corsicans the full rights and liberties of Frenchmen, and allowed Paoli to return. This was welcomed by many Corsicans, including Napoleon, as a

4

generous and enlightened act, and it was an important step in Napoleon's transformation from a Corsican to a Frenchman. Henceforward he was a Jacobin, taking the French side in Corsican politics, and ultimately transferring his allegiance from Corsica to France. He still, however, retained his admiration for Paoli, and defended him in an open letter to the Conservative deputy for Corsica to the Constituent Assembly, who had accused Paoli of dictatorship.

Under the army reorganisation of 1791, Napoleon was promoted first lieutenant and posted to the regiment of Grenoble, stationed at Valence. In August 1791, he again obtained leave, on the plea that his uncle was dying; there was a considerable amount of property coming to the family under his will. In January 1792, the Minister of War sanctioned Napoleon's transfer from the regular army to the post of adjutant to a volunteer Corsica battalion. Ignoring the army order by which all officers had to rejoin their regiments by April 1, 1792, on pain of dismissal, Napoleon secured his election as second-in-command of the volunteer battalion against the faction of Pozzo di Borgo, but only by using violent methods, such as the kidnapping of his opponents.

On Easter Sunday, 1792, riots broke out in Ajaccio between the anti-clerical Jacobins and the fanatical supporters of the non-juring priests. Napoleon hoped to use this opportunity to seize the citadel of Ajaccio, and in the clashes between the volunteers and the town populace used such violent methods of repression, that he was denounced by his opponents to the Corsican deputies in Paris. Pozzo di Borgo raised the matter in the Legislative Assembly. If Napoleon was to secure reinstatement in the regular army, it was high time for him to go to Paris to make his excuses. He arrived there on May 28, 1792.

Experience of the Revolution in Corsica had already

5

given Napoleon a distaste for mob violence, and the scenes which he saw with his own eyes outside the Tuileries on June 20 and August 10 confirmed this impression. There is an elaborate account in his memoirs of the scenes on August 10, which might be suspected of being coloured by his later anti-Jacobin views; but it is confirmed by the letters he wrote from Paris in June and July 1792. Describing the demonstration of June 20, he writes to Joseph: "The Jacobins are lunatics and have no common sense"; "The King showed up well." To Lucien on July 3 he writes: "Every individual is out for his own interests, and will forward them, if he can, by insult and outrage; intrigue is as underhand as ever. All this discourages ambition." Unfortunately there is no letter about August 10, and no evidence that Napoleon was in Paris during the September massacres.

On July 10 the Minister of War had accepted Napoleon's explanation, and reinstated him in his commission, with the rank of captain. He did not, however, take up active duty, since he by now had an excuse for returning to Corsica; the convent in which his young sister Elisa was a pupil was about to be dissolved, and he had to accompany her back to Corsica.

The Girondin government in Paris, with their incredible optimism about the popular support awaiting the revolutionary armies in enemy countries, decided in October 1792 on an invasion of Sardinia from Corsica. Some thousands of 'patriot' troops from Marseilles were assembled in Corsica, where their indiscipline and quarrels with the Corsican volunteers proved to be so troublesome that it was decided to use the Corsicans in a separate, subsidiary attack on the island of Maddalena simultaneously with the main French attack on the capital, Cagliari. Napoleon and his volunteer battalion took part in the Maddalena operation in January 1793.

6

Napoleon succeeded in landing some guns on the island, and came near to reducing the fort and harbour to surrender, when the troops panicked and mutinied and the expedition retreated in disorder. Napoleon in disgust sent a complaint to the Ministry of War about the conduct of the expedition.

As soon as England entered the war against France at the beginning of 1793, suspicion of Paoli's pro-English sympathies was bound to grow and was exploited by his opponents. He had been a friend of Boswell and Dr. Johnson, and is a familiar figure in the pages of the famous *Life of Dr. Johnson*. The rift between the faction of Paoli and Pozzo di Borgo and that of the pro-French Jacobins under the deputy Saliceti, with which the Buonaparte family was increasingly identified, grew wider. Joseph Buonaparte had been a member of the Corsican government which had been defeated in the elections of 1792 by Paoli's supporters, and Paoli himself was suspicious of Napoleon's ambitions. He was reported to have said of him : "You see that young man; he has in him two Mariuses and a Sulla." In February 1793, Saliceti and two other deputies were sent from Paris to supervise Paoli, who was then deprived of his independent command of the Corsican forces, and put under the orders of the headquarters of the Army of Italy.

While Saliceti was negotiating with Paoli, news arrived that the Convention had decreed the arrest of Paoli and Pozzo di Borgo. This precipitate step was the result of a wild denunciation of Paoli by Lucien, Napoleon's young brother, to the Popular Society of Toulon, and it made civil war in Corsica inevitable. Napoleon knew nothing of Lucien's action, and disapproved of it. His first reaction was to try to avert the catastrophe by addressing a petition to Paris defending Paoli and pleading for conciliation. The Convention withdrew its hasty

7

decree at the end of May, but it was too late. Paoli's supporters held Ajaccio and half the island, and Napoleon, after an abortive attempt to seize the citadel of Ajaccio, narrowly escaped capture, and joined Saliceti at Bastia. A Paolist congress condemned the Buonaparte family to 'perpetual execration and infamy'; Letizia and her family were forced to fly into exile, and the Buonaparte property was pillaged. Napoleon made one last but hopeless attempt to raise his supporters in Ajaccio by a naval demonstration, and then accompanied the family to Toulon.

Though the exile meant, in effect, the end of the Corsican period in Napoleon's career, he was still thinking of Corsica. He wrote an appreciation of the situation in Corsica, which was forwarded to Paris, and was instrumental in securing the condemnation of Paoli as a traitor. Paoli retaliated by delivering Corsica to the British fleet, which occupied it until the autumn of 1796, when the defection of Spain from the anti-French coalition temporarily forced the fleet to withdraw from the Mediterranean.

The summer of 1793 was perhaps the most dangerous moment through which the Revolution passed. The expulsion of the Girondin deputies from the Convention on June 2 under armed pressure from the Commune of Paris, raised half the provinces of France, especially the south, in revolt against the authority of Paris and the Mountain. At the end of August, the Girondin faction and the royalists yielded Toulon to the combined British and Spanish fleets. Napoleon was temporarily employed in organising the coastal artillery defences and supplies for the Army of Italy. He also wrote a political pamphlet, the *Souper de Beaucaire*, which, in the form of a dialogue, defended the cause of the Mountain against the Girondins, and denounced the folly of a fratricidal civil war. In August he petitioned the Ministry of War for a transfer to the Army of the Rhine. But the moment of his first great opportunity had arrived, with the siege of Toulon. On September 7, the officer commanding the artillery in the army besieging Toulon was wounded. Saliceti, Napoleon's friend and political patron, was the deputy attached to this army, and reported a few days later to Paris that " chance has helped us well; we have retained Captain Bonaparte, an experienced officer, who was on his way to the Army of Italy, and ordered him to replace Dommartin".

Throughout the siege of Toulon, Napoleon's influence in the operations was quite out of proportion to his rank, even though he was soon promoted lieutenant-colonel. Artillery was the dominant arm; and he had the support of Saliceti, the link between the army and the Committee of Public Safety. The first two commanders in charge of this operation were both incompetent, political generals; the officer nominated to command the artillery never arrived in time, because his orders went astray. When Dugommier, an experienced veteran of the Seven Years' War, arrived from the Army of Italy in the middle of November to take over the command, with General Du Teil, brother of Napoleon's former commander at Auxonne, to command the artillery, they recognised his worth and gave him a fairly free hand. Napoleon had perceived at once the vital point to attack —the fort of Eguillette, at the tip of the peninsula which separated the inner from the outer harbour. Once this was gained, the inner harbour would be made untenable for the allied fleet, and the rest would follow automatically. Napoleon urged an immediate attack on this point, before the English landed, and erected batteries. "Take Eguillette, and you will be in Toulon in eight days."

But the opportunity passed and the siege bogged down.

Barras and Frèron, the deputies sent by the Convention to the south, despaired, and even reported to the Convention that Provence should be abandoned to the invaders. Napoleon had meanwhile dispatched his plan to Paris through Saliceti, and it formed the basis of Carnot's directive to Dugommier. Napoleon, as secretary to the Council of War, drew up the minutes which translated this directive into operational orders. The superiority of Napoleon's plan can be judged by comparison with the numerous other plans urged upon the Committee of Public Safety; it alone concentrates on the decisive point and avoids dispersion of effort. On December 14, the intensive bombardment began, with a simultaneous feint attack on the coastal heights opposite the peninsula; on the 17th, Fort Mulgrave, the English battery covering Eguillette, was captured, and on the following day the English commander, realising the impossibility of holding Eguillette, made the decision to retire and leave Toulon to its fate. Sidney Smith succeeded in blowing up some of the French ships and magazines, but the sudden fall of the city left most of the French fleet and installations intact.

Du Teil and Augustin Robespierre wrote glowing reports to Paris on Napoleon's part in the victory. Writing to his brother, Augustin described Napoleon as an "artillery general of transcendent merit", and includes him in a list of reliable patriots. In February 1794, Napoleon was promoted brigadier-general, and appointed as his aides two young officers, Marmont and Junot, who had become his close friends during the siege.

The government crisis of Thermidor, 1794, and the fall of Robespierre, very nearly cut short Napoleon's career. After Toulon he had become ever more closely associaated with Augustin Robespierre, with whose backing he became, in effect, director of the planning of operations at the headquarters of the Army of Italy. Augustin Robespierre went to Paris to urge on the Committee of Public Safety Napoleon's schemes for an Italian offensive. The memorandum by Napoleon which he took with him is a work of genius, and shows that the conception of his Italian campaigns of 1796–7 had already taken shape in his mind. "If our armies on the frontier of Piedmont take the offensive, they will force Austria to protect her possessions in Italy, and thenceforward their strategy will conform to ours. It is the same with strategy as with sieges—concentrate your fire on a single point. Once the breach is made, the equilibrium is overturned. The rest becomes weaker and the place is taken. It is Germany that must be attacked; once that is done, Spain and Italy fall of themselves. If we obtain great success, we can in the following campaigns attack Germany through Lombardy, the Tessin and Tyrol, while our armies in Germany strike at the heart."

But Carnot was against an offensive in this theatre, and his resentment at the intervention of the Robespierre faction in matters of strategy added to the divisions in the government which precipitated the crisis of Thermidor. Napoleon was thus dangerously implicated in political quarrels, and after the execution of the Robespierres, he was denounced as their 'planner', who had undertaken a secret and treasonable mission to Genoa on their behalf. The deputies Saliceti and Albitte, who had ordered his arrest, held an enquiry which cleared him, and he was released after a few days under arrest. Competent staff officers were completely lacking in the Army of Italy, and Napoleon was soon re-employed at headquarters. He was responsible for the planning of the battle of Dego (September 1794), which successfully countered an Austrian threat to the French communications. Napoleon held the view that a vigorous pursuit after this battle would have gained Piedmont.

At the beginning of 1795, his thoughts turned for the last time to Corsica, when he was appointed to command the artillery in an expedition to recapture Corsica. An indecisive action with Hotham's fleet on March 15 forced the expedition to turn back.

At the beginning of April, Napoleon received the extremely unwelcome news that he had been posted as an infantry brigadier to the Army of the West, engaged in the Vendéan war. This was a political decision. The Committee of Public Safety was suspicious of English influence in Corsica and decided, as a precaution, to transfer Corsican officers from the Army of Italy. On reaching Paris, Napoleon staved off his departure for La Vendée on the pretext of illness, and managed through the good offices of Pontécoulant, a member of the Committee of Public Safety who was interested in the plans for the Italian campaign, to get himself appointed head of the Topographical Bureau of the Committee. Pontécoulant also backed his application to go as head of a military mission to Turkey, but, fortunately perhaps for Napoleon, his patron was dropped from the Committee on September 1. On September 15, Napoleon was notified by the Ministry of War that he had been struck off the list of generals owing to his refusal to obey the order to report to the Army of the West.

It was the crisis of the insurrection of Vendémiaire (October 5, 1795) that not only came to Napoleon's rescue at this juncture but put his feet firmly on the ladder to power. When the new constitution of the Directory was promulgated, the Convention, as its last act, had passed the 'Law of the Two-Thirds', which required that two-thirds of the new assembly should be composed of members of the outgoing Convention. The reaction against the Terror had set the tide of public opinion in

Paris strongly in favour of the moderates and royalists, and the Paris Sections were immediately up in arms against the 'Law of the Two-thirds'. The Sections mobilised 25,000 men, against whom the Convention could oppose barely 5,000. The general in command of the government forces proved himself incompetent and politically suspect. Barras was then given by vote of the Convention command of the Paris troops and the Army of the Interior. As a deputy on a mission in the south, he had met Napoleon in the Toulon days, and as a last resort he called in the man who had so successfully handled the artillery on that occasion. Captain Murat was dispatched to secure the all-important cannon from the artillery-park at Sablons, and, owing to Napoleon's skilful dispositions, the attack on the Tuileries was easily repulsed—by a "whiff of grape-shot".

As the reward for his success, Napoleon was promoted to major-general, and shortly afterwards succeeded Barras as commander of the Army of the Interior. Napoleon was now a personage of considerable power and importance, and he could give his attention to the thoughts of marriage which had already entered his head since his arrival in Paris in May—even when he was so penniless that he had to rely on Junot's success at the gambling table for a square meal. Perhaps it was Joseph's happy marriage in 1794 with Julie Clary, daughter of a Marseilles merchant, that turned his thoughts in this direction. He was fond of Julie's younger sister, Desirée, and there was an understanding, if not an engagement, between them, which seems to have lapsed when he went to Paris. (Desirée later married Bernadotte, and died as Queen of Sweden.) Napoleon actually proposed marriage to Madame Permon, an old friend of his father's, whose daughter Laura later married Junot and became Duchesse d'Abrantès. Madame Permon laughed at the proposal, and pointed out that she was old enough to be Napoleon's mother.

Through his acquaintance with Barras, Napoleon had, even before Vendémiaire, been introduced to the salon of Madame Tallien, Barras' mistress and the reigning beauty of Parisian society under the Directory. There he met Josephine de Beauharnais, thirty-three-year-old widow of Vicomte de Beauharnais, who had been a republican general in 1791, and had been guillotined under the Terror. Josephine herself only escaped through the fall of Robespierre, and was left penniless with her two children, Eugène and Hortense. She, like Beauharnais, came of a wealthy and aristocratic family of Martinique, Tascher de la Pagerie. She had become Barras' mistress for a time, as an easy way of retaining a life of luxury. This fascinating widow, with the elegance of the *ancien régime*, easily captivated Napoleon, who was not without snobbish instincts. At St. Helena, he recalled his first meeting with Josephine. "I was certainly not insensible to feminine charms, but I had never till then been spoilt by women. My character rendered me naturally timid in their company. Madame de Beauharnais was the first woman who gave me any degree of confidence." Napoleon was passionately in love with her; and, moreover, her political connections were valuable. After Vendémiaire he was in a position to offer marriage, and Josephine, with some hesitation, accepted. They were married on March 9, 1796. On March 2, Napoleon had been appointed to the command of the Army of Italy. Henceforth, he was to sign his name 'Bonaparte', instead of the Italian form, 'Buonaparte'.

It has been said that Napoleon owed this appointment to the influence of Barras, who gave it him as a reward for taking over his discarded mistress. But La Revellière, one of the Directors, categorically states in his memoirs that it was the unanimous decision of the Directory on straightforward military grounds. It was, indeed, a natural appointment in view of the situation. Since Prussia and Spain had dropped out of the war by the middle of 1795 through the treaties of Basle, the Committee of Public Safety were free to consider an Italian offensive. Napoleon, as head of the Topographical Bureau, drafted the instructions for the Army of Italy on the lines of his memorandum of 1794. Schérer replaced Kellerman as commander-in-chief, and was given reinforcements from the Pyrenees and the Rhine. In November 1795, Schérer took the offensive and won the battle of Loano; but his campaign was brought to a standstill by bad weather and lack of supplies. Napoleon continued after Vendémiaire to act as adviser to the government on Italian strategy, and wrote a series of memoranda pressing for a renewed offensive. Schérer became so much annoyed by continual prodding from the Directory, which he knew to be inspired by the upstart Bonaparte, that he asked to be relieved of his command, unless his army was increased to 60,000 men. The Directory took him at his word, and decided on the appointment of Napoleon, who himself drafted the instructions for the campaign of 1796. Carnot and his colleagues were finally convinced that only the man who had conceived the offensive strategy could carry it out.

It is clear, even from this brief survey of Napoleon's early career, that he was from the start much more than a professional soldier. His thorough training as an officer did, it is true, provide the foundation for his career, but his interests were as much political and literary as military. At an early age, he had learnt how to judge and handle men in the hard school of Corsican politics. It was his political connection with Saliceti that gave him his first big chance at Toulon. He was a true product of the revolutionary age; a time when the crust of social custom had been broken, and nothing seemed impossible of achievement to men with clear minds and strong wills. His intelligence and character were moulded by the two most powerful influences which inspired the Revolution, the scientific, rationalist spirit of the Enlightenment and the romantic sensibility of Rousseau. The romanticism which is so evident in his early writings is soon overlaid by a colossal, devouring egoism; just as the style of his writing changes from that of Rousseau to the terse, brief Napoleonic style. The language of sensibility appears for the last time in his early letters to Josephine.

Perhaps it would be more true to say that this romantic trait in his character was not extinguished but transformed into a romantic ambition—romantic because it was unlimited, feeding on dreams of a career which was to outdo those of all the heroes of history; not for him the limited ambition of the enlightened despots of the eighteenth century—of a Frederick the Great. The romantic imagination of Napoleon backed by the realism of his intelligence formed a marvellous and formidable combination, which had a magnetic attraction for the men of his own age who had been moulded by the same influences and experienced the same feelings. But what would happen if this balance was upset—if the realism was lost and the imagination became uncontrolled? Moscow and St. Helena, as well as Austerlitz and the Empire, seem to be implicit in his very nature.

Chapter Two

The Italian Campaigns

TO contemporaries Napoleon's Italian campaigns of 1796–7 seemed almost miraculous : a dozen victories in as many months, announced in bulletins which struck the public like thunderclaps. It was a revelation of a new kind of *blitzkrieg*, and it was natural to ascribe it simply to the genius of the commander and the *élan* of the revolutionary armies. But to the military historian it appears also as the logical culmination of changes in the theory of war which had been gradually evolving for half a century.

It was the staff of the old royal army of the *ancien régime* that worked out the new theory between the Seven Years' War and the Revolution. Neither the Revolution nor Napoleon himself contributed any major innovation in theory or weapons, apart from the signal-telegraph and military observation balloons which were introduced in 1793–4. Napoleon developed the former and suppressed the latter as useless. The French flintlock musket of 1777 was unchanged till 1840, and the French artillery designed by Gribouval in 1765 was in use till 1825. But the improved flintlock and bayonet which appeared about 1720, and Gribouval's light and efficient field-guns, together with the introduction of metalled road surfaces, made for greater mobility and fire-power. Infantry could move in smaller formations and still defend themselves against cavalry; the stiff, compact order of battle which made eighteenth-century battles decisive, but easy to avoid unless both sides wanted them, was no longer necessary. Frederick the Great's battles were won by tactical ingenuity on the field of battle, with formations and drill inherited from his father and already becoming antiquated.

While most armies, like the Prussian, remained mesmerised by the tradition of Frederick, and clung to the Frederickian drill, the French staff after the Seven Years' War displayed great intelligence and enterprise in working out the principles of a new offensive warfare, based on the possibilities provided, but not yet exploited, of improved weapons. Bourcet, who was adviser to de Broglie, the French commander-in-chief in 1759, and from 1764 Director of the Staff College at Grenoble, wrote a treatise on *Principes de la Guerre de Montagnes*. He taught the superiority of offensive over defensive strategy, the dispersion of divisions to feed and march, but only at a distance that would enable them to concentrate rapidly for battle; the importance of having a plan "with several branches" to keep the enemy guessing, and of determining, and if necessary changing, the "line of operations". Guibert's *Essai Général de Tactique* of 1772 made a profound impression. He criticised the old, complicated line of battle, and preferred simple battalion columns. He foretold the ending of wars of position by a mobile war of manœuvre, and he wished to free the army of clumsy baggage-trains. "War must feed on war." He was something of a political philosopher, too, and realised that the new kind of warfare required a new kind of soldier. "It would be easy to have invincible armies in a State in which the subjects were citizens."

Du Teil, brother of Napoleon's commander at Auxonne, worked out in his essay of 1778 on *Usage de l'artillerie nouvelle dans la guerre de campagne* the tactics of the new field-artillery, insisting on the concentration of fire-power on the decisive point, and the combined use of artillery and infantry. In 1788, a new drill-book was drawn up, and issued to the army in 1791, laying down clear but flexible instructions for manœuvre in column or line according to circumstances.

Thus, by the outbreak of the Revolution, the French army had a sound and coherent doctrine of offensive strategy and tactics which was being expounded by the staff. Napoleon absorbed this doctrine in his professional training at Valence and Auxonne; it was far more important to him than his reading of military history, which was comparatively superficial, apart from a study of Maillebois' campaign in Piedmont in 1745. His early memoranda are full of echoes from Bourcet, Guibert and Du Teil's writings, and his opening campaign may almost be described as a translation of Bourcet's ideas into fact. This is not to belittle Napoleon's military genius, but only to explain it. He himself said at St. Helena: "I have fought sixty battles, and I have learnt nothing which I did not know in the beginning." And in his remark that "everything is in the execution", he has said the last word on the relation of theory to practice in the art of war.

The first effect of the Revolution was to disintegrate the old royal army. The monopoly of commissions for the *noblesse* created a rift between officers and men which was fatal to discipline. At the outbreak of the war in 1792 whole regiments fled and murdered their officers. The volunteers raised in 1791 were good material, but untrained and undisciplined; the volunteers of 1792 and 1793 were in fact mostly conscripts, as the Departments had to make up any deficiencies in their quota by compulsion. When national conscription was decreed in the middle of 1793 and Carnot took charge of mobilisation, the revolutionary army was gradually forged into a powerful weapon; 800,000 men were equipped and in the field by the beginning of 1794, and the fusion of regular and conscript battalions into the new demi-brigade, which had been delayed for political reasons, was generally adopted.

The industrial mobilisation to equip these large forces was as remarkable an effort as the military conscription. New gun factories were rapidly developed in Paris, and scientists were brought in to organise steel and coal production. Large-scale industry had just begun to develop in France in the 1780s, and it was able to sustain the revolutionary and Napoleonic type of warfare, with its high rate of wastage both of men and material.

The mass emigration of regular officers opened the way for vigorous young leaders from the ranks, such as Masséna and Augereau in the Army of Italy. But there was a desperate shortage of officers with professional staff training capable of commanding above the divisional level. A man with Napoleon's qualifications and background, if he survived the guillotine or a stray bullet, was therefore likely to get high command at an early age.

'To lie like a bulletin' became a proverbial saying under the Empire, and the manufacture of the Napoleonic Legend, started by Napoleon in his bulletins and continued at St. Helena, complicates the task of the historian from the outset of Napoleon's first campaign. At St. Helena he gave a version of his first speech to the Army of Italy, which read: "I will lead you into the most fertile plains in the world. Rich provinces and great cities will be in your power; you will find there honour and glory and riches. Soldiers of Italy, will you fail in courage or constancy?" No official record of this speech exists, and, in fact, Napoleon's first order of the day was in sober and conventional language.

There is also the dramatic but exaggerated account of Napoleon's arrival as commander-in-chief: the young, insignificant general, appointed through political influence, who was at first greeted with derision by the veteran officers of the Army of Italy. In fact, he was already well known to the officers through his connection with the army as a staff officer in 1794-5, and they welcomed him as a commander who would lead them in a successful offensive. Even the Piedmontese commander was aware of his reputation when he was appointed, as 'a brilliant theorist and strategist'. It is worth analysing Napoleon's Italian compaigns in some detail, since they provide, in the application of the basic principles, the model for his later campaigns.

On arriving at Nice on March 27, 1796, Napoleon found Berthier, his chief of staff—the beginning of an association unbroken till 1814—and Masséna and Augereau, two of his divisional commanders. Saliceti, his old patron, had been appointed civil commissar to the army in January, and by raising a loan in Genoa had considerably improved the supply position. Although the army had achieved nothing spectacular since 1792 and was badly fed and clothed, it had become seasoned by continuous campaigning. It had a high proportion of regulars and early volunteers, and its morale and discipline were comparatively good. By combing the rear formations, Napoleon was able to bring its striking power up to 38,000.

He was well aware that there was no love lost between the Austrians and the Piedmontese. The Austrians were suspicious of the traditional Piedmontese policy of playing off France against Austria; they would support Piedmont only with the minimum number of troops to keep her in the field as a buffer between France and Lombardy, and if Piedmont cracked, they would withdraw to Lombardy rather than rescue her. The allied forces, consisting of 30,000 Austrians under Beaulieu on the left wing, resting on the coast, and about 25,000 Piedmontese under Colli (of whom only about 12,000 were available as a striking force), were tough, veteran troops, well-trained in the Frederickian tradition, with competent but elderly officers. Napoleon's plan for the campaign of Piedmont was designed to exploit the weakness of the enemy alliance; he proposed to separate the Austrian and Piedmontese forces, beat them in detail, knock Piedmont out of the war as quickly as possible, and then deal with the Austrians.

Before Napoleon arrived to take command, the French had moved a small force on Voltri, on the coast west of Genoa, to apply pressure on Genoa to provide the loan demanded by Saliceti. Beaulieu was also being urged by the Austrian ambassador to secure Genoese territory, and he interpreted the French move to mean that the main theatre of operations would be on the Riviera coast. He therefore moved considerable forces in that direction and captured Voltri. In so doing, he moved too far from his Piedmontese allies, in face of an opponent as quick in decision and movement as Napoleon, and, in fact, lost the campaign at the start. Napoleon at once saw the possibilities of the situation created by the diversion of the Austrian force, and took the offensive against the Austrian right wing in the mountains. In a series of battles round Montenotte (April 12–16) he inflicted about 6,000 casualties on the Austrians, and Beaulieu was so shaken that he decided to fall back on his base at Alessandria. This left Napoleon free to deal with the Piedmontese, who were broken in the battles of San Michele, Ceva and Mondovi (April 19–23), on which day Colli sued for an armistice. In each of these battles, the French had superiority of numbers, although the total allied forces were equal to the French; a classic example of the skill of the commander in deployment and timing.

Napoleon wasted no time in exploiting the conquest of Piedmont. On April 28 he secured an armistice at Cherasco, which was to last a month, and give him control of the fortresses and line of communication between France and Lombardy. Leaving the Directory to negotiate a definitive peace with Piedmont, he turned to the pursuit of Beaulieu. He failed to catch him south of the natural defence line of the River Po, but by crossing the Po at Piacenza on May 7, well to the east of Beaulieu's main position at Pavia, he threatened his line of retreat. Beaulieu was forced to withdraw quickly across the Adda towards Mantua, and on May 10 the French forced the bridge of Lodi, defeating Beaulieu's rearguard. On May 14, Napoleon entered Milan.

The victory of Lodi was for Napoleon a psychological landmark in his career. At St. Helena, he said : "It was only on the evening after Lodi that I realised I was a superior being and conceived the ambition of performing great things, which hitherto had filled my thoughts only as a fantastic dream."

On May 21, Napoleon received news that peace with Piedmont had been signed, which relieved him of anxiety about his communications. He wrote to Carnot : "Soon it is possible that I shall attack Mantua. If I capture it, nothing can prevent me penetrating into Bavaria." But he never forgot that, from the point of view of grand strategy, the Italian theatre was secondary to that of the Rhine, where the bulk of the French and Austrian forces, of the order of 200,000 on each side, faced each other. All depended on an offensive by Moreau and Jourdan, commanding on the Rhine; failing that, the Austrians, holding the central position with interior lines of communication, could detach sufficient forces from the Rhine to crush the Army of Italy.

The Directory, however, were thinking in different

terms. They had no intention of conquering Lombardy permanently; they wished only to exploit it, and then exchange it for the Rhine frontier when peace came. After Lodi, the Directory instructed Saliceti, the commissar to the army, that the command of the Army of Italy was to be divided; Kellerman was to occupy Lombardy while Napoleon was to move south to plunder Rome and Naples. Napoleon protested vigorously against this decision, and the Directory climbed down. The prestige of his victories and the money which flowed to Paris in consequence gave him the whip hand. While Napoleon and Saliceti encouraged and mobilised the pro-French revolutionary party with promises of independence for Lombardy, they demanded large contributions of money, as well as requisitions for the army, and the surrender of art treasures. Detachments were sent to occupy Leghorn and Bologna, and the Dukes of Parma, Modena and Tuscany, as well as Rome, Naples and Venice, were forced to make armistice agreements and pay ransom. By July, Saliceti estimated that 60 millions of francs had already been levied from Italy. These exactions soon produced disquieting signs of resistance; at the end of May, a rising of the populace in the region of Pavia had to be ruthlessly crushed.

Meanwhile, Moreau was making no headway on the Rhine. In fact, for the remainder of the year the French campaign on the Rhine was frustrated and finally defeated by the skill of the Austrian commander, Archduke Charles. This put Napoleon on the defensive, and exposed him to repeated and dangerous Austrian counter-attacks through the Alpine passes. Fortunately for Napoleon, the Austrians always advanced in isolated corps, which gave him the opportunity of his favourite defensive manœuvre—attacking each corps in turn from a central position.

At the end of May Napoleon had resumed his advance against Beaulieu, who was holding the line of the Mincio. By a feint attack north towards Trent, Napoleon forced Beaulieu to disperse his forces, and then struck against his centre. Beaulieu retreated in disorder towards the Tyrol, leaving a strong garrison in Mantua, to which Napoleon now laid siege. For the remainder of 1796, the main fighting took place in the area of the quadrilateral —the fortresses of Peschiera, Verona, Mantua and Legnago in the plain below Lake Garda—which was also to figure prominently in the wars of 1848 and 1859. It was not the siege of Mantua in itself that forced Napoleon to halt his advance, but the inactivity of Moreau; and the line of the Adige and the quadrilateral were the strongest positions from which to meet the Austrian counter-offensive.

At the end of July, Wurmser, who had replaced Beaulieu, began his advance with 47,000 men in all, divided into three columns—one moving down the west side of Lake Garda, one on the east side and another farther east on to Bassano and Verona. Napoleon was outnumbered, with 42,000 men available, of whom 10,000 were engaged in the siege of Mantua. A dangerous situation developed, when Wurmser threw back Masséna's division east of Garda, and the second Austrian corps on the west side captured Brescia on July 30 and threatened the French line of communications. Napoleon made the courageous decision to abandon the siege of Mantua, sacrificing his siege-train, in order to regain freedom of manœuvre, and if possible defeat the Austrians separately before they could join forces. Wurmser wasted time in reinforcing Mantua, enabling Napoleon to withdraw and concentrate his forces west of the Mincio. Between August 1 and 3, the French attacked south of Garda round Lonato, and forced the Austrians to withdraw northwards. Wurmser,

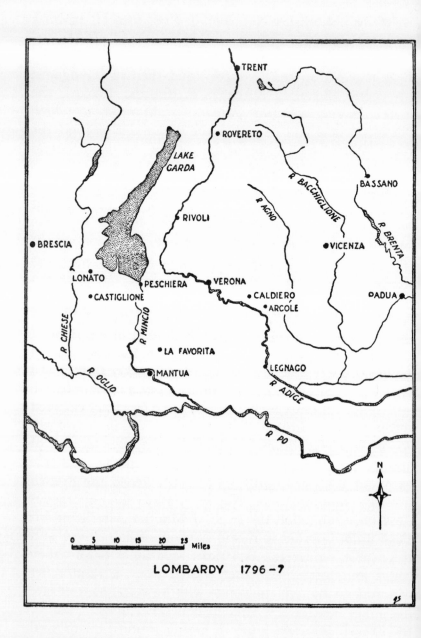

LAKE GARDA

TRENT

ROVERETO

R BACCHIGLIONE

BASSANO

RIVOLI

R AGNO

R BRENTA

BRESCIA

VICENZA

LONATO

PESCHIERA

VERONA

CALDIERO

CASTIGLIONE

ARCOLE

PADUA

R CHIESE

R MINCIO

LA FAVORITA

LEGNAGO

R OGLIO

MANTUA

R ADIGE

R PO

N

0 5 10 15 20 25 Miles

LOMBARDY 1796-7

under the impression that his lieutenant was still holding his ground, advanced west from Mantua to join him without waiting for the third corps to come up, and was caught by Napoleon at Castiglione on August 5 with only 21,000 to the French 27,000. He was decisively routed and had to retreat in disorder to the Tyrol.

Napoleon now had hopes of resuming his advance over the Brenner, but he soon found that Wurmser was reassembling a strong force on the River Brenta, to move on Mantua by the most easterly route. Napoleon decided not to remain on the defensive but to move on Trent, with his whole field force of 32,000, so as to take Wurmser in the rear if he advanced on Mantua. On September 4, he beat the Austrians at Rovereto north of Lake Garda, and captured Trent. On September 8, he took Wurmser's force in the rear, and dispersed it at Bassano. Wurmser lost 6,000 men, and was thrown back westwards, away from his communications. He only narrowly escaped envelopment and capitulation, and took refuge in Mantua.

At the end of October, Moreau retreated to the Rhine, and the Austrians were in a position to send reinforcements to Italy, and make a further attempt to relieve Mantua. Alvinzy, the new Austrian commander, had 19,000 men on the Brenner, and 28,000 men on the Brenta, moving on Trent and Bassano, at the beginning of November. Napoleon had received no reinforcements, and his troops were now depleted and exhausted. Some of the forced marches demanded, and obtained, by Napoleon were almost incredible, especially in the summer heat of the Lombardy plain. Augereau's division once covered seventy miles in forty-eight hours. Their morale was low, and nearly cracked under the strain of this new onslaught. Napoleon was defeated on the Brenta and on November 12 at Caldiero, and withdrew to the central position of Verona.

On the 15th, Napoleon determined on a daring attack on Alvinzy's rear as he moved on Verona—by crossing to the left bank of the Adige and seizing Arcola. As a surprise attack on the Austrian convoys, it miscarried because of the stubborn Austrian defence of the bridge of Arcola. In vain Napoleon tried to urge on his troops to a final effort by advancing on to the bridge with a standard, surrounded by his staff.[1] But after three days of heavy fighting, the balance of numbers inclined to the French side, and Alvinzy retreated towards Bassano. This enabled Napoleon to reinforce the division which was holding the Austrian corps advancing from Trent, and to defeat them at Rivoli, east of Lake Garda. But the Arcola campaign was a purely defensive victory by a narrow margin, and a costly one. Louis Bonaparte, Napoleon's younger brother and aide-de-camp, wrote despondently after Arcola: "The troops are no longer the same, and shout loudly for peace."

With Mantua still holding out and Moreau thrown back to the Rhine, the Austrians still had hopes of recovering Lombardy, and the Directory's overtures to Austria were rebuffed. The Directory decided to make the main offensive from Italy in the campaign of 1797, and to reinforce Napoleon with 40,000 men; but the bulk of them could not arrive before March. Alvinzy was ordered to make another effort to relieve Mantua, and at the beginning of January he advanced again in three columns. Joubert's division to the east of Garda was attacked by Alvinzy, and Napoleon, waiting at Verona to see how the situation developed, soon decided that the main Austrian effort was directed on Joubert. On January 13, Napoleon

[1] The truth of this incident has been denied by F. Kircheisen in his biography of Napoleon. But the recently published letters of Sulkowski, Napoleon's aide-de-camp, give an eye-witness account of it which there is no reason to disbelieve (see M. Reinhard, *Avec Bonaparte en Italie*).

concentrated 23,000 men and 30 guns at Rivoli, and on the 15th he caught Alvinzy there with his infantry and artillery separated. By the evening the rout of Alvinzy was certain, and Napoleon hastened back to meet the column marching from Padua on Mantua. On the 16th this relief force was forced to surrender in the battle of La Favorita, outside Mantua. By the end of January, the Austrians had withdrawn to the mountains and Mantua had surrendered.

At the beginning of March the Army of Italy had increased to 80,000 men, and Napoleon had the choice of advancing over the Brenner or across the Tagliamento to Trieste. When he found that the Archduke Charles, who had replaced Alvinzy, was concentrating to the east in Friuli, he chose the Trieste route, leaving Joubert to advance over the Brenner. By the end of March, he had reached Klagenfurt. The Austrian resistance was ineffective, and they had lost about 13,000 men in their retreat. Joubert had reached Brixen, and was ready to join up with Napoleon in the valley of the Drave. But Napoleon realised that his position, so brilliant in appearance, was in fact precarious. Unless Moreau moved forward from the Rhine, Joubert would be taken in flank from the north. Guerrillas were active in the Tyrol, and there were risings in Venetia on Napoleon's line of communications. In the absence of any news from the Rhine, he wrote on March 31 to the Archduke Charles to propose an armistice. While the Archduke was consulting Vienna, Napoleon pushed on to Leoben (under a hundred miles from Vienna), where peace preliminaries were signed on April 18. France was to keep Belgium, and secret articles further provided that she should keep Lombardy, and Austria should be compensated with the mainland territories of Venice.

Napoleon had received no authority from the Directory

to negotiate; nothing was said in the preliminaries about the Rhine frontier, and the terms contradicted the Directory's policy of exchanging Lombardy for the Rhine frontier. Meanwhile, Moreau and Hoche had started their advance a day after the terms were signed, and Napoleon's negotiation appeared premature. Napoleon wrote to the Directory to justify his action as a military necessity. In any case, the Directory had to swallow the terms. News that peace was imminent had leaked out, and they could do nothing against the public enthusiasm for peace.

The political weakness of the Directory had forced them to abandon, step by step, the control of the military authorities by the civilian government which had been firmly established by their predecessors, the Committee of Public Safety. The formidable 'Representatives to the Armies', appointed by the Convention, had been replaced by commissars with lesser powers appointed by the Directory. Of the two commissars with the Army of Italy, Saliceti had left to conduct the expedition to recover Corsica, and the other was unable to stand up to Napoleon, who accused him of endangering the army in the Arcola campaign by failing to provide supplies. In May 1796, Napoleon had on his own initiative decreed that the troops should receive half their pay in cash, not depreciated paper money—a step which was enormously popular in the army and attached it to himself personally. In October, he had committed the government to recognising a Cispadane Republic of Lombardy, and conferred the civil administration on his military governor.

So far from resisting these encroachments, the Directory decreed in December 1796 the suppression of the office of commissar to the armies, thus leaving the generals a free hand. Napoleon negotiated the Treaty of Tolentino with the Pope (February 1797) entirely on his own initiative. The commissars had been in perpetual conflict with the generals, both in Italy and on the Rhine, and they had not succeeded in providing the Directory with as much money from the occupied territories as the Directory had expected. But the main motive for this decree was political. The Directory were faced with a strong revival of moderate and royalist opposition, and were forced to lean for support on the republican sentiment, which was still strong in the Armies of the Rhine and of Italy. The crisis of Fructidor, and the ultimate fate of the Republic, was foreshadowed.

In the summer of 1797, the fate of Europe for the next twenty years hung in the balance. If a moderate government came into power in Paris, a durable peace was possible, and ultimately a restoration of the monarchy, which would block Napoleon's rise to power. The elections of May 1797 gave the moderates a majority in the legislature, and their representative entered the Directory. Britain, like Austria, was at the end of her tether and ready for peace. In August 1796, Spain had joined France, and the British fleet had withdrawn from the Mediterranean, abandoning Corsica. Ireland was ripe for rebellion, and Hoche's Bantry Bay expedition of December 1796 only narrowly failed, and might be renewed at any moment. In the spring of 1797, Pitt, faced with the naval mutinies at Spithead and the Nore, and a financial crisis, was prepared to make peace, even at the cost of leaving Belgium in French hands, in return for the Cape of Good Hope and Ceylon. In July, Malmesbury was sent to Lille to negotiate with Talleyrand, the new French Foreign Minister. Both the Austrians and the British dragged out peace negotiations through the summer, hoping for a change of government in Paris.

Napoleon was now installed in semi-royal state with Josephine, at the castle of Mombello near Milan; but he took care to keep in touch with the situation in Paris. He was in charge of the negotiations for ratifying the peace preliminaries of Leoben, and his first concern was to secure the downfall of the Venetian Republic. A massacre of French troops at Verona at Easter gave him the excuse for an ultimatum. The Doge in vain tried to avert invasion by agreeing to introduce a democratic, pro-French government. No sooner was it installed than it called in French troops. Austria then occupied Istria and Dalmatia, and France the Ionian Isles. A similar procedure was used to overturn the Genoese Republic, which accepted a French constitution and became the Ligurian Republic. In July, the union of Modena, Ferrara, Bologna, the Romagna and Carrara to the Lombard Republic, now called the Cisalpine Republic, was proclaimed.

Napoleon had been able to push ahead with the organisation of Italy because by now he saw that three of the Directors, Rewbell, Barras and La Revellière, would have to rely on him for aid in a *coup d'état* against the moderate Directors, Carnot and Barthélemy, and the legislative councils. These three Directors were more sympathetic than the others to his Italian policy, and in any case would be in no position, after the *coup d'état*, to oppose a peace settlement on the lines of Leoben. They had first looked to Hoche, but the plan to bring his troops near Paris and make him Minister of War was exposed in the legislature and miscarried. Napoleon then sent Augereau to Paris at the beginning of August to organise the military side of the *coup d'état*. In vain, Thugut, the Austrian Chancellor, sent an envoy to Paris to attempt a separate negotiation with Barthélemy. His envoy reported that "only Bonaparte can make peace, and he can do it on any terms he wants". On September 4 (18 Fructidor) the three 'Jacobin' Directors surrounded

the Tuileries with troops under the command of Augereau, ordered the arrest of Carnot and Barthélemy, and
expelled 200 deputies from the legislature.

After Fructidor, the Directory at once stiffened their
terms to Malmesbury at Lille, and at the end of September the conversations were broken off. The Austrians
now saw that they must settle with Napoleon and make
the best bargain they could. At Udine, after strenuous
discussions, a treaty formally known as Campo Formio,
was signed on October 18, 1797. Austria recognised the
Cisalpine Republic, and the French possession of Belgium and the Ionian Isles. In return, she received the
Venetian territories on the Italian mainland up to the
Adige, as well as Istria and Dalmatia. In a secret article,
she agreed to support the French demand for the left
bank of the Rhine at a Congress to be held at Rastadt,
while France was to help her to secure Salzburg and a
strip of Bavaria.

It was a brilliant peace for France and for Napoleon,
but it laid the seeds of future war. Owing to the prestige
of Napoleon's victories and the internal weaknesses of the
Directory, the French peace aims had been diverted from
the 'natural frontiers'—the Rhine, the Pyrenees and the
Alps—to Italian annexations, which meant further
expansion and war.

Chapter Three

Egypt and the *Coup D'État* of Brumaire

WHEN Napoleon sent Augereau to Paris to lend support to the *coup d'état* of Fructidor, he had deliberately shelved for the time being any attempt to seize power for himself in France. At Mombello, however, he did not disguise his contempt for the 'lawyers' of the Directory. "Do you think that I triumph in Italy in order to benefit the lawyers of the Directory—the Carnots and the Barras?" But he decided that the "pear was not yet ripe'. Time was needed for the French people to become thoroughly tired of the Directory and a crisis which would make them turn to a dictator for salvation.

In the meantime Napoleon felt the danger to his career of an anti-climax after the Italian victories. Immediately after the Peace of Campo Formio, he had been appointed to the command of the 'Army of England', and the Directory invited him to attend the Congress of Rastadt as head of the French delegation before he returned to France. The Congress was called to make peace between France and the German Empire, and its first business was, in effect, to ratify the French possession of the left bank of the Rhine, in return for the cession of Venice. By December 1, agreement had been reached on these points, and Napoleon left for Paris. He was officially welcomed by the Directory with great ceremony, but there was one passage in his speech which sounded ominous. "When the happiness of the French people is established on better organic laws, the whole of Europe will become free." Was this a hint of a further *coup d'état*? In Barras' circle there was talk at this time of reforming the Constitution and strengthening the executive. But Napoleon made no further political move and avoided public appearances. He wore civilian dress, moved mostly in the company of scientists and writers, and was rewarded by election to membership of the Institute (the equivalent of the Royal Society in England). He had correctly anticipated, and allowed for, a slackening of public interest and enthusiasm. "In Paris, nothing is remembered for long. If I remain doing nothing for long, I am lost."

The plan for a direct attack on England did not attract him after the failure of Hoche's attempt on Ireland in 1796. He carefully inspected the preparations which had been started between Brest and Antwerp. Despite the fact that he could count, on paper, on 57 battleships and 50,000 men, and money forthcoming from the occupation of Switzerland and Rome in the spring of 1798, he reported unfavourably on the project at the end of February. "With all our efforts, we shall not for many years obtain command of the sea. . . . Our fleet is today as little prepared for battle as it was four months ago, when the Army of England was projected. . . . The suitable moment to prepare for this undertaking is perhaps gone for ever."

But an alternative project was taking shape in Napoleon's mind—the Egyptian expedition. This was not a wholly original idea. Napoleon had read Raynal's *Histoire des Deux Indes* (1780) and Volney's *Considérations sur la guerre actuelle des Turcs* (1788), in which he wrote: "Only one thing can indemnify France . . . the possession of Egypt. Through Egypt, we shall reach India, we shall re-establish the old route through Suez, and cause the route by the Cape of Good Hope to be abandoned."

35

The importance which Napoleon attached to the possession of the Ionian Isles in the peace negotiations of 1797 shows his interest in the East. In August 1797, he was writing to the Directory "the time is not far off when we shall feel that, to destroy England completely, we must seize Egypt", and also suggesting the capture of Malta. A former French consul in Egypt had urged an attack on India by way of Egypt as early as 1795, and Talleyrand had been interested in this scheme. On February 14, 1798, Talleyrand, independently of Napoleon, wrote a memorandum to the Directory, strongly recommending an Egyptian expedition. On February 23, Napoleon reported to the Directory against the attack on England, and recommended Egypt as an alternative. On March 5, the Directory approved the plan for the Egyptian expedition, and their instructions of April 12 to Napoleon directed him to conquer Malta and Egypt, secure the Red Sea, improve the condition of the inhabitants of Egypt, and to maintain as far as possible good relations with the Porte. This last point was inspired by Talleyrand, who hoped that Turkey might be kept from open hostilities, on the ground that the French were driving out the Mameluke usurpers from Egypt, as the ally and protector of Turkey.

While ships and troops were being concentrated swiftly at Toulon, Napoleon went to Brest to maintain the deception of a campaign against England. Thirty thousand men were to be left on the northern coasts to divert England from the Mediterranean, and attempt a landing later in the year, if possible. After a delay due to a threat of a breakdown of the negotiations at Rastadt, Napoleon sailed from Toulon on May 19. The expeditionary force included, besides 38,000 troops and nearly 400 ships, a 'Commission of Arts and Sciences' consisting of over 150 scientists, engineers and archæologists, fully equipped with libraries and instruments. During the voyage, Napoleon had long conversations with his 'Institute of Scientists'. Junot, his aide-de-camp, was found to be snoring during one of these sessions, and, when woken up, excused himself by saying: "General, it is all the fault of this confounded Institute of yours: it puts everyone to sleep, yourself included." The expedition was planned, not merely as an operation of war, but as the foundation of a permanent colony.

It was a miracle that such an unwieldy and slow-moving force escaped destruction from the English fleet in the open sea. Nelson was watching Toulon, but a great storm, which delayed the sailing of the French fleet, damaged Nelson's ships so severely that he had to retire to Sardinia for extensive repairs. Thus the French were able to land at Malta on June 10, and force the capitulation of the island from the Grand Master of the Order of St. John. The English ministers were still quite uncertain about the destination of the Toulon expedition; they thought of Naples, Portugal or Ireland. They had never taken seriously the French designs on Egypt, and had even suppressed the British consulate in Egypt. Despite the fact that the English agent at Leghorn wrote on April 16 that the expedition was destined for Alexandria, the Admiralty kept an open mind. Only Dundas had an inkling of the truth and sent reinforcements to India.

On June 15, Nelson wrote to the Admiralty: "If the French pass Sicily, I think they intend to seize Alexandria." The news of the capture of Malta determined him to sail direct for Alexandria, where he found nothing and left forty-eight hours before the French arrived. After revictualling in Sicily, he received fresh news off Greece, and returned to Alexandria on July 31. On August 1, he caught the French fleet at anchor in Aboukir Bay, after completing the disembarkation, and annihilated it. Only two battleships escaped out of a total of thirteen.

Nelson returned to Naples, confident that Napoleon and the Egyptian expedition, cut off from their base, were quickly doomed. The news of the naval disaster reached Napoleon on August 13; he concealed his anxieties and proceeded calmly with the occupation of Egypt. On land, he had had quick and overwhelming success. On July 21, at Embabah (the so-called Battle of the Pyramids) he had easily defeated the *corps d'élite* cavalry of the two Mameluke Beys, by forming the French into squares. The Mameluke cavalry numbered about 6,000; their infantry of about 12,000 were an ill-armed rabble, negligible as a fighting force.

Napoleon had issued strict instructions to the army to respect the Mohammedan religion, and to refrain from pillage. His policy was to try to separate the Coptic and Arab populations from the cause of their Mameluke overlords. In Cairo and the provinces he set up native advisory councils. He held long discussions with the ulema of Cairo on Moslem theology, holding out to them the possibility of the whole French army being converted to Islam. He wrote to Mecca, proclaiming his respect for the religion of the Prophet. An Institute of Egypt was founded, and vast plans for the exploration of Egypt put in hand, including the survey of the isthmus of Suez and the archæological investigation of Upper Egypt. To these activities can be traced the discovery of the Rosetta Stone, and the vast *Description de l'Égypte* (1809–28), which laid the foundations of Egyptology. Napoleon's interest in the Suez canal project fired the imagination of the Saint-Simonians and De Lesseps in the 1830s, and made its eventual realisation a French achievement.

Napoleon's attempts to conciliate the native population were only partly successful. The Mamelukes were still stirring up opposition from their desert bases, and Napoleon's desperate shortage of money forced him to levy unpopular taxes and contributions. Nelson's victory at Aboukir had encouraged the Turks to declare war on France on September 9, and when this news reached Egypt, it caused a serious insurrection at Cairo on October 16, which had to be ruthlessly suppressed. In January 1799, Napoleon received news that the Governor of Syria had collected an army for an invasion of Egypt, and he welcomed this excuse for a forestalling attack on Palestine and Syria. His troops were disgusted with the squalor of Cairo, and were losing their morale through inactivity. In his reminiscences at St. Helena, Napoleon tried to represent the Syrian campaign as the prelude to a return to Europe by way of Constantinople, or a march on India. At the time, he was too realistic to entertain seriously such ambitions, far beyond his limited resources. It is true that he wrote to Tippoo Sahib, the pro-French Sultan of Mysore; but he held out no promise of help.

Napoleon set out for Palestine on February 10, 1799, with 13,000 men. The capture of Jaffa (March 7) by storm was disgraced by the massacre of 3,000 Turkish prisoners, on the plea of military necessity, since Napoleon had not sufficient troops and supplies to escort and feed them. Plague was beginning to infest his army. Jaffa had fallen so easily that Napoleon underestimated the difficulty of taking Acre. The first assault, which he undertook without waiting for his siege-artillery to arrive, failed, and after a siege of two months he was forced to retreat (May 20). The factor which baffled Napoleon at Acre was Sidney Smith and his small squadron, which was able to cut Napoleon's sea-communications, and strengthen the garrison with naval artillery and technical experts, among whom the most important was Phélipeaux, the French *emigré* engineer and former fellow-cadet of Napoleon. In reporting the end of the siege, Sidney Smith grandiloquently concluded : "The plain of Nazareth has become the limit of the extraordinary career of Bonaparte."

By the time Napoleon re-entered Cairo, after a difficult retreat, his Syrian expeditionary force had been reduced to 8,000 men. He was immediately faced with an invasion by a Turkish army of 20,000 men from Rhodes. By a masterly concentration of his forces, reminiscent of the best days of the Italian campaigns, Napoleon annihilated the Turks at Aboukir (July 25, 1799). This victory, by wiping out the unsatisfactory record of the Syrian campaign and securing Egypt from any immediate threat, left Napoleon free to consider his return to France. He had never intended to stay long in Egypt : before starting he had told the Directory he hoped to be back before the end of 1798 to resume command of the Army of England. Before he left for Acre he had received disquieting news from a French merchant that Naples had invaded the Papal States. In front of Acre at the end of March, he received the first dispatches from the Directory to reach him through the British blockade. They told him of the renewal of war in Italy, and authorised him to march on India or Constantinople, or bring back his army to Europe. In April 1799, the Directory sent the Brest fleet under Admiral Bruix into the Mediterranean, to try to evacuate part of the army from Egypt. At the same time, they sent instructions to Napoleon (which never reached him) authorising him to hand over the command in Egypt, and return, if he judged it safe to do so. Bruix was delayed at Toulon, waiting for his Spanish ally, and in the meantime the British concentrated such strong forces in the Mediterranean that he was forced, with much difficulty, to retire to Brest.

On August 2, Napoleon obtained copies of French newspapers (obligingly supplied to him by Sidney Smith in the course of negotiations about the exchange of prisoners) which told him of the loss of Italy and the defeat of Jourdan on the Rhine. On August 24 Napoleon sailed from Alexandria in the greatest secrecy. He took with him only a small staff of generals and scientists, in two frigates and two smaller vessels. His successor as commander in Egypt, General Kléber, only knew of his appointment by letter after Napoleon's departure. Napoleon, in his supreme and cold-blooded egoism, was not deterred by any scruples about deserting his doomed and dwindling force, nor by the fact that he had received no definite authorisation from his government to return without a substantial part of his army. On the plane of high politics and strategy, he was clearly taking a bold and correct decision. Egypt could only be secured by victory and peace in Europe, and the crisis had clearly arrived which would bring him to supreme power or to the guillotine.

By hugging the North African coast, Napoleon's small flotilla had evaded the English cruisers. Between Corsica and Toulon they narrowly escaped the attention of an English squadron, which probably mistook them for a coastal convoy. Napoleon landed at Fréjus on October 9, 1799. His journey to Paris, up the Rhône Valley and through Lyons, developed into a triumphal procession of popular enthusiasm and acclaim. General Bernadotte, on hearing of his arrival, advised the Directors that Napoleon should be court-martialled for deserting his army and evading the sanitary laws against plague. The Directors soon realised that nothing of the sort was possible, in face of public opinion. This reaction of public opinion was an index of the unpopularity of the government; Napoleon was remembered only as the victor of Campo Formio, the one man who could restore peace and order to the Republic.

Since Napoleon's departure for Egypt, the fortunes of France had gravely deteriorated. Nelson's victory at Aboukir had precipitated the Second Coalition against France. It brought in the Turks, then Naples, followed by Tsar Paul of Russia, already incensed by the capture of Malta and the French expedition to the Levant, and finally Austria. Jourdan's Army of the Danube had been beaten by the Archduke Charles at Stockach (March 1799), and Suvorov, in command of an Austro-Russian force, had occupied Milan and Turin. Naples and central Italy were lost, and Joubert, the new commander of the Army of Italy, was defeated and killed by Suvorov at Novi (August 15). It is true that by the time of Napoleon's arrival in France, the situation had been largely restored. Masséna had beaten the Russians at Zürich (September 26), and Brune in Holland had forced the Anglo-Russian force under the Duke of York to re-embark (October 18). But a victorious peace was still nowhere in sight.

Internally, the government of the Directory had shown itself to be incurably incompetent, irresolute and divided. Since the *coup d'état* of Fructidor, the Constitution had ceased to function normally; the government could only keep going by alternate blows at the royalists and the Jacobins. As a result of the elections of May 1798, over a hundred deputies were excluded as being too Jacobin (Floreal, 1798). In May 1799, Sieyès entered the Directory, and the elections of May produced a marked swing to the left. There is no doubt that the personal incompetence and corruption of the Directors have been exaggerated, and that the difficulties of their situation have not been sufficiently appreciated. They had inherited from the Convention a fearful legacy of debt and inflation, and they had made repeated efforts to restore the currency, balance the budget and ensure a regular revenue by taxation. But all these efforts broke down through the weakness of the central government and the division of power between the Directory and the Councils. Chronic weakness of finance threatened the payment and supply of the armies, and deserters swelled the bands of brigands which infested whole areas of France.

The idea of a revision of the Constitution to strengthen the executive power was in the air. Sieyès had his own plan, and his aims were shared by men such as Daunou, Roederer and Talleyrand, who were to form the party of the Brumairians, and help Napoleon to power. The behaviour of the Jacobin majority in the Council of Five Hundred strengthened their hands. They voted a Law of Hostages, authorising the imprisonment of relatives of *emigrés*, which recalled the worst days of the Terror; and a progressive income tax which frightened the bourgeoisie and the financiers.

The Jacobin Club was reopened, and in September a resolution to 'declare the country in danger' and set up a revived Committee of Public Safety was only narrowly defeated in the Council of Five Hundred. Sieyès was looking round for a soldier to carry out his *coup d'état*. He had thought of Joubert, but Joubert was killed at Novi. Bernadotte, Jourdan and Augereau were courting popularity with the Jacobins. Moreau was irresolute and lacking in political courage. When he heard of Napoleon's landing at Fréjus, he said to Sieyès : "There's your man; he will carry out your *coup d'état* much better than I."

On arriving at Paris, Napoleon was at first preoccupied with a domestic crisis. He had received news in Egypt of Josephine's repeated infidelities, and had come back fully determined to divorce her. Moreover, he had consoled himself in Egypt with a Mme Fourès, wife of a lieutenant. Her husband had obtained a divorce, and it is quite likely that Napoleon would have married her if she had given him a child. Josephine hurried out of Paris to meet Napoleon on his way, but missed him and arrived in Paris to find the door bolted against her. However, Napoleon's resistance collapsed at the sound of her voice, and there was an immediate reconciliation—much to the annoyance of the Bonaparte family, who detested the influence of the Beauharnais.

It was unnecessary for Napoleon to take any political initiative—he was courted by every faction. Barras, his old patron, was anxious to make use of him; but Napoleon soon realised that Barras and his colleagues wanted to get rid of him as quickly as possible by offering him the Italian command. Moreover, he was aware that Barras was corrupt and despised, and he kept him at arm's length. Jourdan, Augereau and the Jacobins were prepared to offer him a military dictatorship, provided he subscribed to their policies. These he abhorred, and he had no intention of becoming the prisoner of a faction. Roederer and Talleyrand saw him frequently, and were anxious to put him in touch with Sieyès. Though Sieyès, conceited, dogmatic and excessively doctrinaire, was personally uncongenial to Napoleon, he decided to ally himself with Sieyès and the moderates, concealing his intention to make use of them rather than the reverse.

It has been said of Brumaire that "never was a *coup d'état* worse conceived, or worse executed". But it must be emphasised that Brumaire really consisted of two distinct *coup d'états*—first, the days of St. Cloud, which were planned primarily by Sieyès, and the second, in which Napoleon disposed of Sieyès, and so twisted Sieyès' idea of the new constitution as to ensure that supreme power was concentrated in his hands. In the first stage, it suited Napoleon to leave the plans vague, to conceal his objectives; and he was prepared to run considerable risks to preserve legal forms and to create a new government on as broad a base as possible. He did not want a military *coup d'état*; and it would be quite wrong to describe Brumaire as the establishment of a military dictatorship. Nothing would have been easier for Napoleon than to call on the army and throw the parliamentarians into the Seine. The garrison troops of Paris, 8,000 strong, would do whatever he ordered, though the 1,500 Grenadier Guards of the Directory and the Councils were more doubtful. They were Jacobin in temper and had never served under Napoleon. Public opinion was generally on Napoleon's side. As a police spy wittily wrote in a report: "I denounce the public." The Jacobins of the Council of Five Hundred received no support from the people of the Paris faubourgs, who in 1793 had made governments tremble. The confused events of Brumaire must be seen against this background.

On the 10th Brumaire, Napoleon and Sieyès met, and agreed on their plan. By invoking a clause of the Constitution which gave power to the Council of Ancients to move the legislative assemblies from the capital, both Councils were to meet at St. Cloud, and there be induced to vote a new provisional Constitution. Nothing had so far been agreed between Napoleon and Sieyès about the form of the Constitution, beyond the fact that it should consist of an executive of two or three Consuls, and legislative commissions to draft a new Constitution. As for the Directors, Ducos and probably Gohier would follow Sieyès, and Barras and Moulin were to be forced to resign. Fouché, the Minister of Police, was not in the plot, but it was certain that he would sit on the fence and keep his police immobilised. The weak point of the plan, which proved in the event to be ex-

tremely dangerous, was the delay involved in the move
to St. Cloud. First, the Council of Ancients had to be
persuaded, on the pretext of a Jacobin conspiracy, to
vote the move to St. Cloud and the command of the
troops of the capital to Napoleon; on the following day
both councils would meet at St. Cloud. There was a risk
that in the intervening twenty-four hours the opposition
would be warned and given time to organise.

The first part of the plan, on the 18th Brumaire, went
without a hitch. The Council of Ancients voted the
resolution to transfer the Councils to St. Cloud without
difficulty, since the opposition leaders had, by design,
received no summons to the meeting. Napoleon appeared
before the Council, accompanied by a large following of
generals, including the existing commander of the Paris
garrison, and was invested with the command of the
troops. Lucien, Napoleon's brother, who had recently
been elected President of the Council of Five Hundred,
immediately adjourned the Council to the following day
at St. Cloud, on receiving the resolution of the Council
of Ancients. Gohier and Moulin were paralysed by the
inactivity of Barras, who shut himself up, waiting for a
message from Napoleon. Later in the day, Talleyrand
called on him, and put in front of him a draft note of
resignation. Barras signed (probably at the price of a
large bribe), and was immediately escorted out of Paris
to his country estate. Gohier and Moulin refused to
resign, and were put under military guard.

During the evening of the 18th, the Jacobin deputies
of the Council of Five Hundred were free to meet and
concert resistance. They thought of opposing Bernadotte
to Napoleon. Sieyès proposed the precaution of arrest-
ing forty of their leaders, but Napoleon, sure of public
opinion, brushed aside this suggestion. "I do not fear
such feeble enemies." In the morning at St. Cloud he

sensed the danger, aggravated by the delay in preparing the hall for the Council of Five Hundred. Moreover, some of Napoleon's own supporters in the Councils were beginning to have doubts; they had been alarmed by the military display of Napoleon's entourage. A proportion of the less reliable guards of the Councils had been left in their barracks at Paris, and the remainder occupied the courtyard of the palace at St. Cloud, with the troops of the line behind them in the gardens. Even so, the attitude of the conciliar guard was still doubtful. There was a general feeling of nervousness among the conspirators. Bourrienne, Napoleon's secretary, remarked to a friend as they crossed the Place de la Concorde, the scene of Louis XVI's execution: "My friend, tomorrow we shall sleep at the Luxembourg, or we shall finish here."

At one o'clock, the Council of Five Hundred met in stormy mood, and resolved that all the members present should swear an oath to maintain the Constitution. In the Council of Ancients, the opposition complained that they had received no summons to the meeting on the previous day, and demanded explanations of the reason for the move to St. Cloud. By four o'clock, Napoleon felt that the situation was slipping out of control, and determined to appear before the Councils himself. He harangued the Council of Ancients, but his speech became so incoherent that Bourrienne persuaded him to withdraw, saying to him: "General, you don't know what you're saying." He insisted on proceeding immediately to the Council of Five Hundred, accompanied only by two grenadiers of the conciliar guard. He was greeted with cries of "Death to the tyrant"; "Down with the dictator!" Several Jacobin deputies surrounded him, seized him by the collar and shook him violently. Almost fainting, Napoleon was rescued by Murat and a detachment of grenadiers. From the Jacobin majority came the dreaded shout of "Outlaw him!"—which had been heard at Robespierre's downfall. If Lucien had not resisted all attempts to remove him from the President's chair and refused to put the vote, the decree of outlawry would have been passed and Napoleon would have been abandoned to his fate. Eventually Lucien sent a message to say that, unless the session was interrupted within ten minutes, he could no longer answer for the consequences.

Meanwhile, Napoleon had called for his horse, and rode along the ranks of the conciliar guard, saying: "I went to inform them of the means of saving the Republic. They answered me with dagger-blows. Soldiers, can I count on you?" In his nervous excitement, he had scratched his face with his nails, and the blood gave some semblance to the story of the daggers. The troops of the line were incensed against the Council, but the conciliar guard were still hesitant and hostile. Napoleon sent an officer and ten men to rescue Lucien, whose appearance in the courtyard, and presence of mind, finally saved the situation. He denounced the 'minority of assassins', and concluded with a dramatic gesture, which won over the grenadiers of the conciliar guard. Pointing a sword at the breast of his brother, he cried: "I swear an oath to kill my own brother if he ever attacks the liberty of the French people." Napoleon immediately ordered Murat to enter the Council Hall with a column of grenadiers, but added that he wished for no excesses: "I do not want a drop of blood to be shed." At the appearance of the grenadiers with fixed bayonets the deputies fled, many of them climbing out of the windows. At seven o'clock the Council of Ancients voted the nomination of three provisional Consuls—Napoleon, Sieyès and Ducos. Late at night, Lucien collected his supporters in the

Council of Five Hundred—not more than a hundred—
to ratify the decision of the Council of Ancients.

Napoleon, on his return to Paris, issued a proclamation
which repeated the fiction of his attempted assassination,
and omitted mention of the all-important part played by
Lucien. The capital had remained perfectly quiet, and
the announcement of the provisional Consulate was
greeted with enthusiasm. The provinces received the
news equally quietly, except in a Jacobin area of the
south-west; though, curiously enough, the most unfavourable reaction was in the Armies of the Rhine and
Italy. It was this overwhelming majority of public
opinion in favour of Napoleon that really made the
parliamentary opposition ineffective. If the affair at St.
Cloud had been better handled, there need have been
no resort to force. As it was, Napoleon could in an ex-
tremity have relied on the troops of the line to overcome
the scruples of the conciliar guard; the whole significance
of the crisis at St. Cloud, and Lucien's intervention, lay
in Napoleon's desire to preserve legal forms as far as
possible, and appeal, not to the troops of the line, but to
the conciliar guard, to protect the members of the
Councils from the minority of 'assassins'.

Chapter Four

France under the Consulate

THE moderate politicians who had voted for Napoleon as provisional First Consul had no intention of
helping him to absolute power. They looked confidently
to Sieyès to produce a Constitution which, though
strengthening the executive power, would provide sufficient checks and balances to safeguard parliamentary
and individual liberties.

In long and often heated discussions between the
three Consuls and the legislative committees appointed
by the Councils, Sieyès gradually unfolded his plan,
based on the principle of 'Authority from above, confidence from below'. In concrete terms, this meant that
popular election by universal suffrage should be limited
to drawing up local and national lists of 'notabilities'. The
electors in each commune would draw up a list of one-
tenth of their members; one-tenth from the communal
lists formed the departmental electors who chose
one-tenth to form the national list. From these lists a
senate, recruited by co-option, would nominate the
members of a tribunate to propose laws and a legislative
'jury' to pass them. A 'Grand Elector', nominated for
life but subject to recall by the Senate, would appoint
and dismiss two Consuls, one for foreign and one for
internal affairs, each with his own independent administration. Central and local government officials would be
selected by the Consuls from the national and departmental lists.

It was an ingenious scheme for neutralising democracy,

securing the political survival of the Brumairians and en-
suring against a dictatorship. The idea of a tribunate and
'a constitutional jury' or guardian of the Constitution had
already been put forward by Sieyès in 1795 in the debates
on the Constitution of the Year III, and an executive of
'Consuls' and 'Prefects' had been adopted in the Constitution of the Roman Republic of 1798.

Napoleon made no objection to Sieyès' proposals for
the electoral system and local government, which he welcomed as strengthening the executive, but he reacted
violently to the idea of the 'Grand Elector', whom he
described as 'a fatted pig'. Roederer acted as go-between,
and Talleyrand arranged a meeting between Sieyès and
Napoleon which ended in complete disagreement. Finally,
at a meeting of the three Consuls and the legislative
committees, called by Napoleon, Daunou was commissioned to draft a constitution, in which he restored the
system of direct election, made the First Consul incapable of commanding the army or of re-election, and subjected him to the votes of his two colleagues. In the final
debates on this draft, Sieyès' system of lists of notabilities
was restored, and Napoleon secured the all-important
point that the First Consul could decide alone, the
Second and Third Consuls being purely subordinate.
The Consuls were to hold office for ten years, and were
to be re-eligible.

Napoleon completed his *coup d'état* against Sieyès by
the way in which the Constitution was adopted and the
three Consuls nominated. The legislative committees
were induced to sign the draft Constitution in his presence, and at the last moment he proposed that the Consuls should be nominated by Sieyès, instead of being
selected by vote. He was afraid that Daunou might secure
the vote for the Third Consul, and he knew that Sieyès
would have no option but to nominate Napoleon's candi-

dates, Cambacérès, an able and cautious lawyer, and Lebrun, suspected of being a royalist. Sieyès received as compensation the Presidency of the Senate, with power to co-opt his colleagues, and the grant of a national estate, which effectively destroyed his popularity. Owing to the illegal manner in which the Constitution was adopted and put into force before it was submitted to a plebiscite, the lists of notabilities were not ready until 1801, and in fact all officials were nominated by the First Consul, and the members of the Tribunate and the Legislature by the Senate. When the Constitution was proclaimed in the streets, a woman turned to her neighbour and said, "I have not heard a word. What is in the Constitution?" "There is Bonaparte," was the reply. In the plebiscite, completed in February 1800, three million voted for the new Constitution; fifteen hundred dissented.

Napoleon was well aware that his régime could only establish itself by delivering the goods desired by the mass of the French people—a victorious peace and internal stability. For the first few months after Brumaire, there was no confidence that the Consulate would last. Napoleon might fail or be killed in battle; the new administration had yet to prove by its achievements that it was something different from the government of the Directory. The most pressing problem was finance. The Directory had left a Treasury practically empty. Gaudin was called to the Treasury immediately after Brumaire, but the important reforms which he set in train could not produce results for at least a year, and in the meantime Napoleon was forced to resort to loans in order to finance the campaign of 1800. A troublesome opposition immediately appeared in the Tribunate, headed by Daunou, the President, and other Brumairians, disappointed by the autocratic character of the new Constitution. But it was largely an opposition of philosophers and intellectuals, with no support in the country. Napoleon, in his irritation, declared : "We have a dozen or fifteen metaphysicians who ought to be thrown into a pond." During Napoleon's absence in the Marengo campaign, they grumbled and intrigued and canvassed possible successors to Napoleon, such as Carnot, Moreau and the Duc d' Orléans.

The first courier from the battlefield of Marengo brought news of a defeat, but the hopes of the opposition disappeared, when the news finally arrived of a decisive victory. Because of its political importance, Marengo was always officially placed high in the list of Napoleonic victories; but the records were carefully suppressed. Napoleon knew what risks he had taken and how narrowly he had escaped disaster. The campaign was one of Napoleonic strategy stretched to the limit of safety. Napoleon dared not displace Moreau in the command of the Army of the Rhine, and the Army of Reserve which was being concentrated at Dijon numbered less than 30,000 men, mostly raw conscripts and short of artillery. With these, reinforced by a corps detached from the Army of the Rhine, he proposed to make the difficult crossing of the Alpine passes, and take the Austrian commander, Mélas, in the rear while he was besieging Masséna's Army of Italy in Genoa. The bulk of the Army of Reserve passed over the Great St. Bernard, and, after being held up for a week by the Fort of Bardo, below Aosta, on June 2 Napoleon entered Milan. He had deliberately rejected the obvious course of marching directly to the relief of Masséna, in favour of the more daring objective of cutting Mélas' line of retreat. But on June 4, Masséna signed an armistice and evacuated Genoa. Napoleon had to hasten his advance to the west, and in his anxiety to cover all possible lines of retreat for the Austrians, dangerously stretched out his forces, sending two divisions under

Desaix to the south of the Po, and one to the north. On June 14, he unexpectedly found himself in contact with the main Austrian force; at the start of the battle he had only 22,000 men and 20 guns against 30,000 Austrians with 100 guns. He immediately sent orders recalling his dispersed divisions, but only Desaix with one division, which had been delayed by bad roads, was able to arrive in time.

Napoleon's troops were already retreating in disorder when the unexpected arrival of Desaix's division on the Austrian flank, and a well-timed charge by Kellerman's cavalry, turned the Austrian advance into a rout. Desaix was killed at the head of his division; for a moment the whole Napoleonic career had depended on Desaix's determination and the state of the roads in Lombardy. Mélas lost his nerve and signed an armistice the next day, abandoning north Italy as far as the Mincio. But Austria was not yet reconciled to a general peace, and it was only the decisive victory of Moreau at Hohenlinden on December 3, 1800, that determined the Emperor to sign the Peace of Lunéville (February 9, 1801). This treaty restored, and even slightly increased, the French gains at Campo Formio.

The period July 1800–May 1803, when Napoleon was able to give his attention to the internal reorganisation of France, is one of the most important in the whole of French history. For good or ill, the institutions—financial, legal, administrative and ecclesiastical—which were to form the framework of nineteenth-century France were laid down. It would be wholly superficial, of course, to ascribe these achievements solely to Napoleon : the myth of his omniscience and omnicompetence has been a gross exaggeration.

The work of the Consulate was, in the main, to achieve the reforms already projected during the Revolution. In the Council of State, which, under the chairmanship of Napoleon, hammered out the legislation of the Consulate, and in his Ministers and Prefects, Napoleon had able collaborators and experts. Napoleon's contribution was to get things done; for the first time since 1789 (with the possible exception of the great Committee of Public Safety of 1793-4), France felt the impulse of a powerful, unified will. As Napoleon said of the ex-revolutionaries whom he recruited for his government: "There were good workmen among them; the trouble was that they all wanted to be architects." And the success of the Consulate was in direct proportion to Napoleon's success in making his government both civilian and national rather than military. Napoleon insisted that "it is not as a general that I am governing France : it is because the nation believes that I possess the civil qualities of a ruler". He attracted to his government the ablest men, regardless of their past. Former servants of the monarchy, like Gaudin and Portalis, rubbed shoulders with ex-revolutionaries like Merlin de Douai, Treilhard and Thibaudeau. Among the outstanding Prefects were Jean Bon St. André, former regicide and member of the Committee of Public Safety, and Mounier, leader of the royalist right in the early days of the States-General of 1789.

One of the most important institutions which Napoleon took over from the Directory, and developed, was the Secretariat of State. Napoleon turned this into the Ministry of State under Maret, which became a central registry, enabling Napoleon to supervise the separate ministries and departments without allowing them any collective responsibility. In finance, the first and fundamental reform of the Consulate, the creation of a centralised administration for the assessment and collection of taxes, had been attempted by the Directory in 1797 with only partial success. At last the Consulate was strong enough to reverse the fatal decision of the Constituent Assembly, which, by putting the collection of taxes in the hands of autonomous local authorities, had made the yield from direct taxation slow and uncertain. Collectors of taxes were now required to make a deposit in advance of a proportion of the estimated yield of the taxes; and by the end of 1800 the tax-returns were up to date. These reforms were the work of Gaudin, a financial bureaucrat of the *ancien régime*. In February 1800, the Bank of France was founded; it was at first an independent corporation, and its constitution was drafted by Perregaux, one of the leading Paris bankers. It assisted the government, in return for the handling of the tax-collectors' deposits, government pensions and interest on government loans. In 1803, it was given the monopoly of the issue of bank-notes.

In local administration, as well as finance, the Consulate reversed the practice of the Revolution, and returned to the centralisation of the Bourbon monarchy. The law of 1790, which replaced the old provinces of France by new administrative areas, the Departments, had deprived the central government of any effective control over the elected local authorities. By the law of February 1800, Prefects, appointed by the First Consul, were to be in sole charge of the Departments. The elected councils of Departments, cantons and communes were reduced to advisory functions, and mayors were to be nominated by the central government. The Prefects exercised, in their own sphere, as ample an executive authority as did the First Consul; linked by signal-telegraph with Paris, they were directly subject to the control of the central government. As Tocqueville pointed out in his *Ancien Régime et la Révolution*, the Prefects were a revival of the Intendants of the *ancien régime*. Centralisation, the creation of the Bourbon monarchy, was temporarily destroyed by the Revolution, and restored in 1800.

The Civil Code, issued in 1804, and renamed Code Napoléon in 1807, was the realisation of a project conceived at the outset of the Revolution. In 1792, the Convention appointed a drafting committee, which made rapid progress and produced a plan for a Code of 779 Articles. In 1796, a new plan for a Code of 1,104 Articles was produced. In all, five plans were discussed before the final Code was begun in 1800. Such a Code, dealing with the rights and relations of persons and property, was an obvious and urgent need. In 1789, there was nothing approaching a state of legal unity of the French nation. There were no less than 366 local Codes in force, and a fundamental division between north and south. In the south, property rights were based on written Roman law, the Code of Justinian; in the north, on teutonic customary law. This main division was overlaid and complicated by feudal custom, Canon Law and royal ordinance. The Revolution had brought a drastic upheaval in the property-system of France. It had swept away feudal privilege, and had redistributed a vast amount of land by the nationalisation and sale of the lands of the Church and the *emigré* nobility. The new situation urgently required to be defined and stabilised.

What was to be the basis of the new system—an abstract natural law, ignoring the traditions and prejudices of the past, or a choice between the existing systems of southern Roman law, customary law of the north, or feudal inheritance? The Code of 1804 is a compromise between these principles, reflecting in its emphasis the changing trend of opinion since 1789. The plan of the Convention represented the high-water mark of the philosophic, rationalist influence. It recognised the equality of persons, civil marriage, divorce on grounds of incompatibility, adoption, inheritance of illegitimate children if recognised by the parents and equal division of property among the heirs. It was hostile to Roman law, which enforced the despotic authority of the parent and gave absolute freedom to dispose of property by bequest; and inclined more to customary law, which was regarded as more liberal, because it limited paternal authority and safeguarded the division of inheritance in the family. From 1795 onwards, a reaction in favour of Roman law is perceptible, and a return to traditional juristic concepts, away from the rationalism of the Enlightenment.

In the final draft of 2,287 Articles the reaction to Roman law is still more marked, and reflects the influence of Tronchet and Portalis, two eminent jurists of the *ancien régime* appointed by Napoleon to the drafting committee.

In the eighty-four sessions of the Council of State in which the drafts were discussed, Berlier and Thibaudeau, ex-revolutionaries, defended customary law; Napoleon, Portalis and Cambacérès represented the reaction to Roman law. Hence the compromise which preserved the main revolutionary principles of equality, but modified them in accordance with the reactionary trend of the Consulate. The paternal authority of Roman law was restored, and the subjection of married women. Grounds for divorce were severely restricted; adulterous wives could even be imprisoned by their husbands. Property, up to a quarter of the whole, could be bequeathed away from the family. The recognition of illegitimate children was discouraged. These provisions were, to some extent, a necessary reaction against the moral laxity of the period of the Directory, resulting from the breakdown of the social order in war and inflation. The general character of the Code reflects the ideas of the middle class, who had benefited from the Revolution. It emphasised heavily the rights of individual property, and, above all, it reassured the owners of national lands, by confirming the revolutionary land-settlement.

From the strictly legal point of view, Napoleon's contribution was unimportant. Esmein, the French legal historian, says that "interesting as his observations occasionally are, he cannot be considered as a serious collaborator in the great work". Substantially, it is the work of the professional jurists, and probably it would have been much the same without Napoleon's interventions. But he was the driving force which pushed it through; and he presided at thirty-six out of the eighty-four sessions of the Council of State devoted to the Code. Thibaudeau, a reluctant admirer of Napoleon, records that "there was originality and depth in his lightest word".

On the other hand, the Concordat with the Papacy (1801) was conspicuously the personal policy of Napoleon, carried through in the face of opposition from the majority of his advisers, the assemblies, the generals, who were still mainly anti-clerical and even militantly irreligious. When Napoleon came into power, the religious question opened by the Revolution was still unsolved and a cause of grave internal weakness. The Civil Constitution of the Clergy, passed by the Constituent Assembly in 1791, had been condemned by the Pope as uncanonical, because it subjected the bishops and clergy to popular election. A schism resulted in the French Church between the Constitutional Church, which accepted the oath to the Constitution, and the non-juring bishops and clergy. The Convention had ended by persecuting not only the non-juring clergy but catholicism as such, and had provoked civil war in the catholic west—Brittany and La Vendée. Robespierre had realised the political danger of the religious war, and had tried, in his *Cult of the Supreme Being*, to find a formula which would soften the religious strife. After his fall, the official policy of the

59

Republic was one of toleration and neutrality towards the different religious sects, varied by outbursts of persecution against non-juring priests suspected of treasonable royalism, and attempts to foster new cults of rationalistic religion, such as La Revellière's cult of Theophilanthropy.

Napoleon shared the Voltairian scepticism of his contemporaries, educated in the anti-clericalism of the Enlightenment; but his experience of government in Italy and Egypt had soon taught him the political importance of religion. In his dealings with the Papacy in 1797 he had refused to follow the Jacobin anti-clerical policy of the Directory; in Egypt, he had studiously respected the religion of Islam. In defending the policy of the Concordat, he maintained that "society is impossible without inequality, inequality intolerable without a code of morality, and a code of morality inacceptable without religion". "In religion, I do not see the mystery of the Incarnation, but the mystery of the social order." "Men who do not believe in God—one does not govern them, one shoots them." "The people need a religion; this religion must be in the hands of the government."

Apart from these general considerations of an acute but cynical realism, Napoleon saw the immediate advantages of a religious settlement. The reports of his Prefects and his police confirmed his impression that, whatever the attitude of the bourgeoisie and the intelligentsia, the peasants were still obstinately attached to their churches and their priests. Even in intellectual circles, religious scepticism was no longer the undisputed, fashionable doctrine. The religious revival, allied with the literary romantic movement and a counter-revolutionary political theory, which was to reach its zenith in the period of the Restoration, was already challenging the atheism of the Enlightenment. Bonald, Chateaubriand and Fontanes were the leaders of an intellectual movement which

60

traced the anarchy of the Revolution to the decline of religious faith and authority. The *emigré* nobility were already abandoning scepticism and returning to religious orthodoxy.

A Concordat with the Pope would drive a wedge between royalism and catholicism, finally pacify La Vendée and reassure the buyers of Church lands. A settlement based on the schismatic, constitutional Church, or on protestantism, would bring none of these advantages. Only a comprehensive agreement with the Pope would suffice. As Napoleon pointed out : "Fifty *emigré* bishops in English pay are the present leaders of the French clergy. Their influence must be destroyed, and for this I must have the authority of the Pope." Napoleon also had in mind the advantage of a Concordat in extending French influence in the catholic populations of Italy, Belgium and the Rhine provinces.

Two days after the battle of Marengo, a new Pope, Pius VII, elected at a conclave in Venice, reached Rome. Napoleon, before he left Italy at the end of June 1800, sent him a message through one of the Lombard bishops that he wished to negotiate for a Concordat, stipulating only that there must be a complete renewal of the French episcopate and a recognition of the sale of Church lands.

It was not until a year later, July 1801, that agreement was reached, after protracted bargaining. The Concordat recognised the Roman Catholic religion as the "religion of the majority of Frenchmen" (not, as the Pope had pressed for, the 'established' or 'dominant' religion), and guaranteed liberty of worship, subject only to the maintenance of public order. The schism between the constitutional and the non-juring clergy was to be ended by the resignation of all existing bishops and the appointment of a new episcopate. The right of the First Consul to nominate, and of the Pope to institute, bishops was recognised. The French government undertook to pay the salaries of bishops and clergy, thus securing the implicit recognition that the sale of Church lands in the Revolution was irrevocable. In the event, the schism was not completely healed. Thirty-eight of the ninety-three non-juring bishops refused to resign or acknowledge the Concordat, and some of them maintained a dwindling congregation in France, known as the 'Petite Église'. The Pope refused institution to twelve former constitutional bishops, nominated by Napoleon.

The way in which the Concordat was finally passed as a law of the French state in April 1802 further diminished the advantages which the Pope had hoped for. It was presented as part of a general 'Law of Public Worship', which regulated protestantism and other religious sects as well as catholicism, and Organic Articles were added, without consulting the Pope, which reasserted gallican principles and subjected catholicism to minute governmental and police regulation. Even so, the anti-clerical majority in the Tribunate and Legislature reacted strongly against the Concordat. The law had to be withdrawn after the first discussion; and it was only after the Tribunate had been purged and reorganised, and after the Peace of Amiens had given Napoleon overwhelming prestige, that it finally passed. The generals signified their displeasure at the official Te Deum to celebrate the Concordat by forcibly turning the priests out of their seats at Notre Dame; and General Delmas commented to Napoleon that evening : "A fine monkish trick. The only thing missing was the 100,000 men who gave their lives to suppress all that."

The institution of the Legion of Honour (May 1802) was also the personal act of Napoleon, opposed by most of his advisers in the Council of State, and passed only by narrow majorities in the Tribunate and Legislature. The

Orders and decorations of the monarchy—the Saint-Esprit, St. Michel, St. Louis—had been abolished by the Convention, as relics of privilege and contrary to equality. The Revolution did, however, favour some sort of national recognition for outstanding services to the country, and occasional 'civic crowns' were awarded by decree to individuals. But no regular system had been instituted, and it was still an open question at Brumaire. As First Consul, Napoleon granted 'swords of honour' to members of the army. In 1802, he brought forward a comprehensive project for a 'Legion of Honour'. There were to be sixteen 'cohorts' and the different ranks—grand officer, commander, chevalier—were to be granted varying scales of life-pension. The members were to be selected by a Grand Council, presided over by the First Consul. This latter point was the important one, in Napoleon's mind. The 'national list' of 'notabilities', invented by Sieyès, had been drawn up by the end of 1801. Napoleon disliked the idea of a privileged body which was independent of himself, and was determined that the grant of any privilege or distinction should be under his control. In defending his project in the Council of State, he occasionally revealed the counter-revolutionary trend of his thought, and confirmed the suspicions of his opponents. "I do not believe the French love liberty and equality. They are not changed by ten years of revolution. They are like the Gauls, proud and fickle : they have only one sentiment, honour." When Thibaudeau objected that decorations were 'toys', Napoleon replied : "You are pleased to call them 'toys'; well, it is with toys that mankind is governed."

The reforms of the Consulate, considered as a whole, look both ways. From one aspect, they are a continuation of the Revolution; from another, a surreptitious return to the institutions of the Bourbon monarchy. They confirmed and secured the national gains of the Revolution in equality, legal and administrative unity, the career open to talents. In this sense, Napoleon's claim to represent the Revolution is justified. For him and for the mass of the French workers and peasants, the social and administrative aims of the Revolution were far more important than the bourgeois aim of political liberty. The Revolution of 1789 had been, not one but three simultaneous revolutions—social, administrative and political. In 1800, the French people were prepared to abandon the political revolution in order to consolidate the other two.

Moreover, Napoleon, like Mirabeau in 1790, did not regard the Revolution as incompatible with monarchy. Mirabeau, in his secret correspondence with the court, had urged the King to continue the work of Richelieu, and lead the Revolution, by completing the destruction of feudalism and modernising the State. In Napoleon's opinion, the fall of the throne had been due to the 'vanity' of the bourgeoisie and the feebleness of Louis XVI. There were certain features of the Bourbon monarchy which he admired. In the early days of the Consulate, he described the 'old administration' as "the most perfect that ever existed. . . . While conserving every useful innovation produced by the Revolution, he would not reject the good institutions which it wrongly destroyed." In 1809, he was to say : "From Clovis to the Committee of Public Safety, I embrace it all." The Bourbon dynasty had failed to rise to the occasion; it was open to Napoleon "to pick a crown out of the gutter". He saw no reason why a "fourth dynasty of France" should not establish itself, based on the changes brought about by the Revolution.

The logic of the situation, as well as Napoleon's concealed ambition, led irresistibly to the establishment of the hereditary Empire. The regicides, the bourgeoisie and the peasantry, who had put Napoleon into power, could never feel safe so long as the survival of the régime depended solely on Napoleon's life. If he was assassinated or killed in battle, they were threatened with a return to Jacobin anarchy or a Bourbon restoration. Louis XVIII, in his Declaration of Verona in 1797, had given no guarantee that he would not demand the return of the lands of the Church and the *emigrés* to their former owners. Roederer records in his memoirs a conversation with Napoleon as early as August 1800, in which he urged upon Napoleon a hereditary succession as the only possible solution. Napoleon wished to be free to nominate or adopt his heir. He did not fancy any of his brothers as his heir; and it was a long time before he could bring himself to divorce Josephine in order to beget a son. When his brother Lucien launched a pamphlet entitled *Parallel between Cæsar, Cromwell, Monk and Bonaparte*, in November 1800, which hinted at the hereditary solution, he was disavowed and dismissed from the Ministry of the Interior. It was only after a son, Charles, was born to Louis and Hortense, the daughter of Josephine, in October 1802, that Napoleon could solve the problem by adopting the infant Charles as his heir.

The more firmly the Consulate became established, the more desperate became the plots of the royalist and Jacobin opposition; and each successive plot gave Napoleon the opportunity to eliminate his opponents and demand an extension of his powers. In the early days of the Consulate, the royalists had hopes that Napoleon would act the part of General Monk, and eventually restore the monarchy. He had negotiated an amnesty on generous terms with the royalist leaders in La Vendée, and a large number of *emigrés* had been allowed to return to France. But when Louis XVIII wrote directly to Napoleon, urging a restoration of the monarchy, he was curtly rebuffed. Napoleon replied: "You must not expect to return to

France; it would mean marching over a hundred thousand corpses." On December 24, 1800, Napoleon escaped by seconds the explosion of an infernal machine in the Rue Niçaise on his way to the opera. This attempt at assassination was the work of Georges Cadoudal, an ex-Vendéan royalist leader, but Napoleon insisted on ascribing it to the Jacobin terrorists, some of whom had been arrested a few days before. A law of proscription was forced through the Senate, under which 130 Jacobins were condemned to deportation.

The political opposition of the assemblies rose to its height over the passage of the Concordat at the end of 1801. But Napoleon found a way to strike at the Tribunate. Under the Constitution, one-fifth of the membership of the Tribunate was due to be renewed in 1802, but the procedure for renewal was not specified. Under pressure from the government, the Senate nominated the members due for retirement, and in this way twenty of the most prominent members of the opposition were removed. The Tribunate was then induced to reorganise itself into three sections—for legislation, internal affairs and finance—and henceforward its debates were deprived of all life. The opposition of the intellectuals was denied any means of influencing public opinion. A strict censorship of the press and the theatre had been taken over from the Directory and tightened up. In 1803, the section of the Institute devoted to Moral and Political Science was suppressed; Madame de Staël, whose salon was a centre of opposition, was banished from Paris.

The outburst of popular enthusiasm aroused by the passing of the Concordat and the signature of the Peace of Amiens (March–April 1802) gave Napoleon the opportunity to secure the Consulate for life. The Senate first proposed that the Consulate should be extended for a further ten years; but Napoleon, by an able manœuvre, took the matter out of their hands by insisting on a plebiscite. The plebiscite, prepared by the Council of State, asked the electorate to vote on the Consulate to Napoleon for life. The official results gave $3\frac{1}{2}$ million votes in favour; 8,000 dissented. Napoleon followed this up by inducing the Senate to make important modifications to the Constitution by the procedure of a *senatus-consultum*.

The First Consul could now present a successor for confirmation by the Senate and negotiate treaties without submitting them for approval. A new Privy Council was created, encroaching on the functions of the Council of State, which had proved too independent for Napoleon's liking. The legal powers of the Senate were increased; it could revise the Constitution by *senatus-consultum*, dissolve the Legislature and Tribunate, nominate the Consuls. But at the same time the servility of the Senate was assured. The First Consul was to preside over the Senate, which could only co-opt candidates presented by the First Consul. It could act only on resolutions presented to it by the government. The independence of individual senators was undermined by two innovations. The First Consul could award 'senatoreries', national estates, up to one-third of the number of senators; and senators were no longer debarred from holding administrative posts. The electoral system was also changed, superficially in a more democratic direction. Instead of the system of the 'national list', which had never, in fact, been put into operation, there were to be cantonal assemblies, elected by universal suffrage, who chose members of the electoral colleges of arrondissements. These in turn chose the members of the electoral colleges of departments, but only among the 600 most highly taxed citizens, who sat for life, and nominated candidates to the Senate and Legislature. The President and up to twenty members of

67

the departmental colleges were to be nominated directly by the First Consul.

The constitution of the life-consulate of 1802 gave Napoleon practically the powers of an absolute monarch; it only remained to add the façade of the imperial crown. The opportunity for this step came in 1804, with the Cadoudal plot and the execution of the Duc d'Enghien. The only internal focus of opposition left in France was that of the malcontent generals, who were moved mainly by jealousy of Napoleon. The obstinately republican and anti-clerical officers of the Army of the Rhine had been mostly got rid of by sending them to reconquer San Domingo, where many of them died of fever. Bernadotte had narrowly escaped arrest for complicity in a military plot emanating from the headquarters of his Army of the West; but he had proved himself repeatedly to be a man of words not deeds. There remained Moreau, sulking in retirement since his victory at Hohenlinden.

With the renewal of war with France in 1803, Georges Cadoudal had persuaded some of the English ministers to support a scheme to seize Napoleon and carry him off to England. Assassination was not officially mentioned—a rather thin pretence to salve the conscience of the English officials who connived at the plot. Cadoudal hoped to bring together Pichegru, the exiled republican general, and Moreau, and at the right moment to bring over to France a Bourbon prince, preferably the Comte d'Artois. An ex-Jacobin, Mehée de la Touche, who was in the plot, turned informer, and gave the French government an inkling of the conspiracy. The Ministry of Police had been suppressed in 1802, when Fouché was dismissed for opposing the life-consulate; and the organisation of counter-espionage had become less efficient, though Fouché still supplied Napoleon with information from his private agents. In January 1804, the arrest and interrogation of Vendéan royalists revealed that Cadoudal and Pichegru were in Paris, and that a Bourbon prince was expected to land in France at any moment. Moreau was arrested, and admitted that he had conferred with Pichegru. He was condemned to two years' imprisonment, a sentence which Napoleon commuted to exile. Cadoudal and Pichegru were both captured in Paris; Pichegru was found strangled in his cell. Meanwhile the police had collected information about the activities of the Duc d'Enghien, grandson of Condé, at Ettenheim, on the borders of Alsace. They reported that he was accompanied by Dumouriez, the ex-Republican general, now in the service of England; Dumouriez had, in fact, been confused with an *emigré* called Thuméry.

Napoleon, whose nerves were undoubtedly worn down by the continual threat of assassination, determined that only a calculated act of violence would put an end to the Bourbon plots. His mind reverted to the Corsican conception of the vendetta, by the rules of which an attempt at murder entitled the victim to retaliate by killing a member of the rival clan. He gave orders that Enghien should be seized on the territory of the Duke of Baden. The interrogation of Enghien did not reveal evidence of his complicity in the Cadoudal plot, but he admitted his intention to invade Alsace as soon as Austria declared war. On March 21, 1804, he was shot as an *emigré* in English pay. The infringement of neutral territory was a flagrant breach of international law; but Enghien was legally liable to the death sentence if he had been captured in France or in enemy territory.

Napoleon always viewed the execution of Enghien as an act of policy; and in his will at St. Helena he asserted that, in the same circumstances, he would do it again. It certainly had the effect of stopping organised plots against his life by the Bourbons or foreign governments.

Although the famous comment "worse than a crime—a blunder" was attributed to Fouché, and Talleyrand afterwards managed to convince Louis XVIII that he had no hand in the affair, it is probable that both of them strongly urged the arrest and execution. By making Napoleon the accomplice of the regicides, it finally ruled out the possibility of a restoration of the monarchy, and left the way open for the establishment of the hereditary empire. The official argument was that a hereditary succession would put an end to attempts at assassination, since the death of Napoleon would no longer alter the form of government. In May 1804, the Senate proclaimed, subject to ratification by plebiscite, that the "government of the Republic is confided to a hereditary emperor".

With a prophetic gesture, Napoleon's great contemporary, Beethoven, struck out the dedication of his Eroica Symphony to Napoleon, when he heard the news of the proclamation of the Empire. The heroic and constructive period of the Consulate was over, to be followed by the sombre, sterile magnificence of the Empire.

Chapter Five

The Peace of Amiens and the Third Coalition

WHEN Napoleon landed at Fréjus in October 1799, the second coalition against France was already beginning to collapse. The success of Masséna in Switzerland and Brune in Holland in September led to mutual recriminations among the allies, and the Tsar Paul withdrew his troops in disgust. Napoleon took the earliest opportunity to detach Russia from the coalition. Knowing that Malta was the Tsar's obsession, especially since he had been elected Grand Master of the Order of the Knights of St. John, Napoleon offered to hand over the island to the Tsar if it became untenable as the result of the British blockade. After Marengo, he offered to return Russian prisoners without ransom. When Malta capitulated to the English in September 1800, the Tsar's maniac resentment led him to change sides and revive the Armed Neutrality of the northern powers against England. In January 1801, he sent an envoy to Paris to sign a treaty with France, and gave orders for an attack on India through Central Asia. Napoleon was delighted with the turn of events in Russia, but his hopes were dashed by the assassination of Paul in March 1801, and the reversal of his policy by his successor, Alexander.

Austria had already been forced to terms by the successive blows of Marengo and Hohenlinden, and signed the Peace of Lunéville in February 1801. Peace between England and France was not possible till the question of

Egypt had been decided. Napoleon was reluctant to abandon his hopes of saving Egypt, and he made repeated efforts to equip a naval expedition. The threat of invasion of England from the northern coasts of France was revived and Spain induced to invade Portugal. When a French fleet finally sailed in January 1801, it was forced to take refuge in Toulon. At the end of June 1801, Cairo was captured by the English forces under Abercrombie.

Pitt had come to the conclusion that peace must be made. There was no further chance of action on the Continent. England was war weary, and needed at least a breathing-space to build up her industrial and commercial strength; the Armed Neutrality had caused a panic on the wheat-market, and the price of wheat rose to 150s. a quarter in April 1801. The crisis over Catholic Emancipation enabled Pitt to resign and leave the peace-making to a stop-gap ministry under Addington. Negotiations began in March 1801 through the French agent in London for the exchange of prisoners, and the Preliminaries of London were signed in October after it had become clear that Egypt was lost to France. Of her colonial conquests, England was to keep only Ceylon and Trinidad, and to restore Malta to the Order, the Cape to Holland and Egypt to Turkey. The independence of Portugal and the Ionian Isles was to be guaranteed, and France was to evacuate Naples. The definitive Treaty of Amiens, signed on March 25 by Spain and Holland, as well as England and France, added minor amendments to the Preliminaries. In return for an international guarantee of the Order, England undertook to evacuate Malta within three months.

Pitt defended the Treaty as "very advantageous and, on the whole, satisfactory". But even before the Preliminaries had been confirmed by the Treaty, public opinion in England had turned against the peace.

Malmesbury commented on the Treaty: "Peace in a week, war in a month." The City had hoped that it would be followed by a renewal of the free-trade treaty of 1786, which would open the French market to English exports; they found that France intended to continue a protectionist policy which would exclude English commerce from the whole coastline under their control. English exports actually declined in 1802–3. The acquisition of Louisiana by purchase from Spain, and the expedition to San Domingo, roused fear of another French colonial empire. Within a few months of the signing of the peace, Napoleon had annexed Piedmont and Elba, secured his election as President of the new Italian Republic, intervened in Germany to arrange the suppression of the free cities and ecclesiastical territories, invaded Switzerland to impose a constitution, and found excuses to continue the occupation of Holland.

When Lord Whitworth was appointed ambassador in Paris in September 1802, he was instructed to answer no enquiries about the evacuation of Malta. The English government already had in mind the retention of Malta as compensation for the expansion of France in Europe, on the ground that the *status quo* implied in the Peace of Amiens had altered. In international law, this was a poor case, since the independence of the Italian, Dutch and Swiss Republics had been guaranteed, not by the Peace of Amiens, but by the Treaty of Lunéville, to which England was not a party. Napoleon could put them in the wrong by demanding the fulfilment of the Treaty of Amiens to the letter. As Castlereagh said, when it came to the final rupture: "It will be difficult to convince the world that we do not fight solely for Malta." In October 1802, the Foreign Secretary, Hawkesbury, sounded Russia about an alliance to resist French aggression; and at the opening of Parliament, supplies were voted for strengthening the army and navy.

Then, in January 1803, an official French statement on Sebastiani's mission to Egypt quoted him as saying that "6,000 French troops would suffice to reconquer Egypt". It seems that Napoleon intended by this reminder to put pressure on England to fulfil the treaty; but Whitworth had already sent alarmist reports that France intended to reconquer Egypt, and the English government seized on it as an excuse to declare that Malta would be retained until the *status quo* of 1801 was restored. Napoleon was provoked to a violent scene with Whitworth, in the presence of the other ambassadors, on March 13. This has often been represented as a deliberately staged attempt to force a rupture with England; but shortly afterwards Whitworth reported that "it is certain that the First Consul has no desire to go to war". Napoleon admitted to his stepdaughter, Hortense, that "Talleyrand told me something which put me in a temper, and this great gawk of an ambassador came and put himself in front of my nose".

Napoleon had no desire for immediate war; he realised that his fleet was not ready and his colonial projects would be sacrificed. The conditions now laid down by the English—Malta for ten years, Lampedusa outright and the evacuation of French troops from Holland and Switzerland—were followed by an ultimatum on April 26. Napoleon countered by a proposal of Russian mediation, which was refused, and Whitworth left Paris on May 12.

A great deal of ink has flowed on the question of the rupture of the Peace of Amiens. Technically, the English government was in the wrong and broke the terms of the treaty by refusing to evacuate Malta. From the first, they regarded the Peace as a 'breathing-space' and an 'experimental peace'. Some French historians, notably Sorel, have sought to justify Napoleon by arguing that England was never really prepared to leave France in possession of Belgium; on that assumption, he can be represented as waging a series of defensive wars against England, since he was bound by his position as 'heir of the Revolution' to maintain the natural frontiers. But it is clear that, both in 1797 and in 1801, England was prepared to recognise the French possession of the natural frontiers, provided that French expansion went no further. What was impossible for any English government to accept was a complete destruction of the balance of power in Europe and a French hegemony of the Continent; just as later but similar threats had to be resisted from the Germany of William II and Hitler. A power which dominated the Continent could organise the shipbuilding resources of Europe, challenge England's sea-power and so threaten her very existence.

It was exactly this aim that Napoleon had in mind. As he said to his Minister of Marine : "It will take us at least ten years; after that time, with the help of Spain and Holland, we may perhaps hope to challenge the power of Great Britain with some chance of success." If it is true that Napoleon was in no hurry to resume war with England so long as the peace proved profitable to his schemes, he never made the slightest concession to make the peace work. It is idle even to speculate whether this or that action on his part could have averted war. As a French historian, Vandal, so concisely puts it : "It is impossible to say if the task was beyond the capacity of his genius; it was certainly beyond the capacity of his character."

The unlimited ambition which was in his nature expanded with every new opportunity. In 1802, the decay of the European state-system under the shock of the Revolution seemed to invite French intervention and encroachment everywhere. The Empire of Charlemagne was not only taking shape in Napoleon's imagination, but seemed to be emerging of itself from the ruins of dynastic feudalism. France, 'la grande nation', with its 28 millions of homogeneous population, was the largest and best organised state in Europe, bursting with the dynamic forces released by the Revolution. Moreover, Napoleon felt instinctively that "between old monarchies and a young republic the spirit of hostility must always exist. In the existing situation every treaty of peace means to me no more than a brief armistice; and I believe that, while I fill my present office, my destiny is to be fighting almost continually." The Peace of Amiens could only be an armistice, because its terms avoided the main issue; the English and the French imperialism could not live side by side.

It has often been said that Napoleon's preparations for the invasion of England between 1803 and 1805 were a blind to enable him to assemble and train the Grand Army, which was really intended for the overthrow of the Continental powers. Napoleon himself was the first to produce this explanation, to cover up the failure of the invasion. He is reported to have said in the Council of State as early as January 1805 that the Boulogne camp was a ruse to deceive the Continental powers. But it is impossible to read his correspondence for this period, with its constant and almost frenzied attention to the problem of invasion in all its details, without being convinced that he really meant to invade, at any rate in 1805. One may doubt whether he would ever have attempted a crossing of the Channel in barges unescorted by warships. The assembling of the barge-flotilla had been begun before the Peace of Amiens, and it was then regarded by Napoleon as a means of menacing England, rather than as a feasible means of invasion. The flotilla was immensely expanded in 1803–4, and at its peak the project envisaged 2,000 boats of all kinds, to transport nearly 100,000 men and their equipment. There is little doubt that, once landed, they could have captured London, as there were barely 100,000 regular troops in the whole of Britain, and the militia forces raised by Pitt would have had little military value against Napoleon's veterans. But it is possible that Napoleon never intended the flotilla to cross by itself, and that he maintained it as a potential threat, pending the time when his naval forces could make a serious attempt to secure command of the Channel for an escorted crossing.

The idea of a combined operation of the fleet with the flotilla first appears in a letter of Napoleon to Admiral Ganteaume in December 1803. In the spring of 1804, he issued detailed instructions to Admiral Latouche-Tréville, commander of the Toulon squadron. He was to elude Nelson's blockade of the Mediterranean, join Villeneuve, commander of the Rochefort squadron, and enter the Channel. "Let us be masters of the Straits for 6 hours and we will be masters of the world." Latouche-Tréville, by far the best of the French admirals, died in August 1804, and for some months the plan of a combined operation seems to have been in abeyance.

It was revived early in 1805, owing to the entry of Spain into the war at the end of 1804. Pitt had become convinced that Spain was about to declare war, and determined to forestall her by seizing the Spanish treasure-convoy; this precipitated open hostilities in December 1804. The French ambassador in Madrid reported—over-optimistically—that Spain could fit out thirty ships of the line in a few months. Napoleon now developed his grand design by which Villeneuve, who now commanded at Toulon, should sail for Martinique, after picking up a Spanish squadron, and there meet Ganteaume with the Brest, Rochefort and Ferrol squadrons. Having forced

77

the English fleet to disperse in defence of the colonies, the combined fleet would then return with temporary command of the Channel, to cover the crossing of the flotilla.

After a false start due to bad weather, Villeneuve sailed on March 30, 1805, and succeeded in eluding Nelson. He reached Martinique on May 14. Nelson, uncertain whether the Toulon squadron had sailed west or east, to Egypt, did not obtain definite information till April 18 that Villeneuve had passed through the Straits of Gibraltar. By June 4, after a fast passage, Nelson was in the West Indies. Meanwhile, Ganteaume had been unable to break the English blockade of Brest. Villeneuve, having waited the stipulated forty days for Ganteaume, and being alarmed by news that Nelson was near him, set sail for Ferrol. Nelson was able to send a fast ship to inform the Admiralty, which ordered the squadron off Ushant to stop Villeneuve entering port. After an indecisive battle off Finisterre, Villeneuve was able to put into Corunna. Nelson reached Gibraltar on July 18, and moved northward to join the squadron off Ushant.

Napoleon's scheme had begun well, but it had failed to disperse the English fleet, as he hoped, and Villeneuve had lost the lead which he had gained at the start. Napoleon was not aware of the concentration of the English fleet; he thought Nelson had returned to the Mediterranean. If Villeneuve with thirty ships could join Ganteaume at Brest with twenty ships, they could still defeat the English and cover the crossing. Villeneuve was instructed accordingly on July 16, but permitted, in the case of an unforeseen event, to retire on Cadiz. On August 14, he was at sea again, but, on sighting five ships of the line, he turned south and took refuge in Cadiz. By the irony of fate, the ships that were sighted were French, the Rochefort squadron, and Villeneuve had lost the last chance; at this moment there were only seventeen English ships in front of Brest. Even so, it is doubtful if Villeneuve could have arrived in the Channel in time.

Napoleon had been waiting at Boulogne since August 3. On August 23, he wrote to Talleyrand : "There is still time—I am master of England." But the day before, his Minister of Marine had begged him not to order Villeneuve north, as it would mean certain destruction. As there was still no news of Villeneuve, Napoleon on August 24 dictated the orders to Berthier for the march to the Danube. The disaster of Trafalgar, when Villeneuve emerged from Cadiz on Napoleon's orders to sail for Naples, confirmed the basic inferiority of French and Spanish sea-power, of which Villeneuve was so acutely aware.

Napoleon could see the disastrous effect of the Revolution on the French navy, but throughout his career he could not bring himself to accept the consequences. In the American War of Independence, the French navy had been the equal of the British, in construction and personnel; but the wholesale emigration of experienced officers and the confinement of the French ships to harbour owing to the systematic British blockade, had seriously lowered the standard of French seamanship and strangled the functioning of the ports. On the other hand, Nelson had brought to perfection in Trafalgar the new tactics, which were the counterpart at sea of the Napoleonic land-battle, of attacking in column and breaking the enemy line, instead of fighting in line ahead. Shortly before Trafalgar, Villeneuve had written : "We have obsolete naval tactics; we only know how to manœuvre in line, which is what the enemy wants." Napoleon's grand design might have succeeded against a less skilful opponent; but at sea it was Nelson who applied the Napoleonic strategic and tactical principles, and Napoleon who ignored them.

79

If it is true that Napoleon intended to invade England and only abandoned the attempt reluctantly, it is equally true that the camp of Boulogne could also be used as a springboard of attack on the Continental powers. Such an alternative purpose was in accordance with his basic strategical principle of a central position from which to strike at either of two opposing forces. He regarded the formation of a third coalition against France as almost inevitable; it was merely a matter of time and opportunity. In fact, it was only made inevitable by his own repeated encroachments and aggression. If he had recognised the principle of a balance of power in Europe, instead of pursuing the aim of a French hegemony of Europe—an empire which was more than French, more than Carolingian, in fact an empire which was universal in the sense of the Roman Empire—he could have averted a hostile coalition. But the very disunion of Europe which made a coalition difficult tempted him with the mirage of a universal empire.

Austria was financially exhausted, and only wished to be left alone to consolidate the dynastic Habsburg territories amid the ruins of the Holy Roman Empire. She was suspicious of Russia's designs on Turkey and Poland, and had no wish to draw her further into central Europe. Prussia, decadent, spineless and selfish, persisted in the neutrality which she had found profitable since the Peace of Basle in 1795. The bait of the acquisition of Hanover could be used by Napoleon to keep her neutral. Russia wavered between a western policy which would make her Napoleon's rival as the arbiter of Europe and an eastern policy of isolation and partition of Turkey. Her occupation of Corfu and her designs on the Straits aroused the suspicions of England.

It was Tsar Alexander's ambition to pose as the arbiter of Europe that led to the cooling of relations between

France and Russia and the beginnings of Anglo-Russian co-operation. His closest advisers were the anglophil chancellor, Woronzoff, whose brother was Ambassador in London, and Czartoryski the Pole, whose one aim was the restoration of a united Poland under Russia; he regarded a Franco-Russian alliance as fatal to these hopes. Alexander was offended by Napoleon's occupation of Hanover and Naples, after the renewal of war with England, and took the French garrisons in Naples as a threat to Corfu and Greece. After the Sebastiani report, this move looked like a return to Napoleon's designs on the Turkish empire. Alexander was further affronted by Napoleon's demand for the recall of the Russian ambassador in Paris in 1803, because of his anti-French intrigues. Hence it was that Russia alone of the Great Powers reacted violently to the execution of Enghien. The Russian court went into mourning, and a protest was sent to Paris against the violation of German territory. Talleyrand's reply, which compared the Cadoudal assassination plot with the murder of Tsar Paul, was never forgiven by Alexander, and it made the rupture complete. In September 1804, a Russian mission was sent to London to concert measures with Pitt. In May 1804 Prussia, and in November 1804 Austria, signed conventions with Russia, but these were purely precautionary and contingent on further French aggression.

It was the coronation of Napoleon as King of Italy and the annexation of Genoa to France that precipitated the formation of the coalition. These were clear infringements of the Treaty of Lunéville, and drove Austria to join Russia and England. In January 1805, it was announced that the Italian Republic was to become a hereditary kingdom; in March, Napoleon accepted the crown for himself. He tried to lull the suspicions of Austria by explaining that he only accepted it temporarily, because of the refusal of his brothers Joseph and Louis. In April 1805, the Anglo-Russian Convention was signed in St. Petersburg. The objects of the alliance were stated to be the liberation of the territories acquired by Napoleon since the Peace of Amiens. In a secret article a further aim was envisaged, in case of a successful war : Holland was to get Belgium, and Savoy and Genoa were to be given to Piedmont. In June, Genoa voted for annexation to France; and in August, Austria adhered to the Anglo-Russian Convention. Napoleon offered Prussia an alliance and the acquisition of Hanover in August, but she preferred neutrality. On the other hand, Napoleon secured alliances with Bavaria, which was threatened by Austria's territorial consolidation in South Germany, with Württemberg and with Baden.

On September 11, an Austrian army of 60,000 under General Mack invaded Bavaria, while a much larger force had been sent to Italy under the Archduke Charles. Mack's intention was to fall back on the Russian advance-guard under Kutusov, but he had completely miscalculated Napoleon's movements. He insisted that Napoleon could not put more than 70,000 men across the Rhine, and that he could not reach the Danube in less than eighty days. In fact, Napoleon's first columns had left Boulogne on August 26, and by the end of September he was across the Rhine with 190,000 men. By evacuating Naples, he provided Masséna, commanding in Italy, with just sufficient forces to keep the Archduke Charles in check; he also evacuated Hanover, and summoned Bernadotte's corps of occupation southwards to join the Grand Army. Before he was aware of the danger, Mack found himself enveloped at Ulm, and forced to surrender with 50,000 men (October 20). Kutusov, now in command of the Austro-Russian forces, skilfully evaded Napoleon's pursuit, at the cost of abandoning Vienna, which Napoleon entered on November 14. He opened peace negotiations with Austria, but the Emperor Francis stood firm.

Kutusov had received reinforcements which brought his force up to 90,000 men. Owing to wastage and dispersion of his forces in occupation duties, Napoleon's striking force was already inferior; if Prussia decided to join the coalition and further Russian reinforcements came up, his position would be critical. In order to hasten Bernadotte's march south from Hanover, Napoleon had taken the risk of ordering him to march through the principality of Anspach, which was Prussian territory. This incident inclined Frederick William towards the war-party, and Alexander, arriving in Berlin at the end of October, persuaded him to sign the Convention of Potsdam (November 3), committing Prussia to armed mediation. But Frederick William, still anxious to sit on the fence, insisted on a time-limit of December 15 for Napoleon's answer, and a Prussian envoy was dispatched to his headquarters.

But Prussian intervention came too late. Napoleon, unaware of the Potsdam agreement, but sensing the danger, had tempted Alexander into risking a decisive battle by a deliberate show of weakness. He wrote to the Tsar, who had now joined his army, had superseded Kutusov as commander-in-chief, and selected an incompetent Austrian general as his chief-of-staff. Alexander's aide-de-camp was sent to interview Napoleon on November 30, and he reported that Napoleon was weak and could be decisively defeated. Napoleon moved as if to retreat, and on the morning of December 2 the allied army advanced on Austerlitz, stretching out their line to cut off Napoleon's right wing. As soon as Napoleon saw that the centre of this position, the heights of Pratzen, had been weakened, he seized it and cut the allied army in two.

The day ended in the most decisive of all Napoleon's victories. With 73,000 men against 87,000, he inflicted a loss in killed, wounded and prisoners of 27,000; the French casualities were about 8,000. Moreover, the wreck of the Austro-Russian army was completely disorganised and demoralised. Alexander, shaken and humiliated, agreed to Francis' making an armistice and a separate peace. By the Peace of Pressburg (December 27), Austria lost Venetia, Tyrol and Vorarlberg, in exchange for Salzburg. By recognising Bavaria, Württemberg and Baden as independent kingdoms, she lost her last foothold in Germany; and she had to pay a large war indemnity. The Prussian envoy, detained in Vienna by Talleyrand till the news of Austerlitz arrived, hastened to sign an alliance with France, by which Prussia annexed Hanover, in exchange for Neuchâtel and Anspach.

Having ruined the coalition in 1805 by her selfish neutrality, Prussia proceeded in 1806 to challenge Napoleon single-handed. Napoleon had no wish to fight Prussia, and genuinely wanted an alliance with her, provided she was prepared to enter into his system as a vassal state like Spain. But he drove her desperate by heaping humiliation on her, until she threw discretion to the winds and courted military and political suicide. When Frederick William made trouble about ratifying the alliance, Napoleon forced a harsher treaty on him in February 1806, which obliged him to surrender part of the Duchy of Cleves, and close his ports to the English. The formation of the Confederation of the Rhine in July 1806, by which sixteen German princes renounced the Holy Roman Empire and attached themselves to Napoleon as Protector, frustrated the hopes of a hegemony of Germany, which had induced Prussia to seek the French alliance since 1795.

Frederick William was also alarmed by the peace

overtures which both England and Russia were making to Napoleon in the summer of 1806. With the death of Pitt in January 1806, Fox and Grenville had come into office, and Fox, always an admirer of Napoleon, was disposed to try appeasement. On July 20, the Russian envoy signed a treaty by which Russia recognised the cession of Sicily, for which Ferdinand of Naples was to be compensated with the Balearic Islands. Napoleon hoped to use this treaty to force England to terms on the basis of existing possession, provided that England recovered Hanover and France kept Sicily, with compensation for Prussia and Ferdinand. But the agreement on the Balearic Islands in the Russian treaty alarmed the English government, and they drew back. Meanwhile, Yarmouth, the English envoy in Paris, had secretly informed the Prussian government that Hanover was to be restored, and on August 9 Prussia decided to mobilise. This in turn encouraged Russia at the beginning of September to refuse ratification of the treaty. As late as August 17, Napoleon gave orders for the Grand Army, which had remained in Southern Germany since Austerlitz, to return to France. These were cancelled on September 3, and a Prussian ultimatum demanding withdrawal of French troops across the Rhine was sent on October 1.

With their Russian and Saxon allies, the Prussians could draw on a total of a quarter of a million troops, and their striking force of about 130,000 men was roughly equal to Napoleon's. Napoleon had never yet had to fight the Prussians, and it was still thought that the army of Frederick the Great would be more than a match for him. But none of the developments in strategy and organisation which had produced the Napoleonic warfare of lightning movement had touched the Prussian army; it remained a slow-moving professional army, with aged officers and enormous baggage-trains. The result was a foregone conclusion, but it was made easier for Napoleon by the refusal of the Prussians to remain behind the Elbe and wait for Russian support. They advanced into Thuringia in three columns, with the vague aim of threatening the French line of communications from the Rhine. Napoleon, on the other hand, had left the Rhine lightly held, and concentrated his forces to the south-east round Nuremberg. The moment he learnt of the Prussian advance from the Elbe, he moved swiftly north-east, and then wheeled to the west to cut the Prussian communications. Too late, the Prussians decided to retreat northwards, and on October 24, Napoleon with 95,000 encountered Hohenlohe's secondary force of 40,000 at Jena, while Davout with 26,000 held and finally routed the main Prussian army at Auerstadt.

After this double victory, a new feature of Napoleonic warfare appeared in this campaign—the relentless cavalry pursuit, which completed the disintegration of the Prussian army. By October 25, the French were in Berlin, and by the middle of November most of the Prussian fortresses had surrendered and the king was forced to take refuge in Königsberg. Broken by the collapse of his army, he had sued for peace soon after Jena; but Napoleon, on reaching Berlin, abandoned the idea of a quick settlement with Prussia. He was enraged by the documentary evidence he found there of Frederick William's negotiations with Russia for a coalition against him, and as it became clear that the Russians were preparing to fight him in Poland, he preferred to occupy Prussia as a base of operations against Russia and a bargaining-counter in negotiations for a general peace. Napoleon therefore stiffened his terms, which Frederick William refused to ratify, after they had been accepted by his representatives in Berlin on November 16; and the Prussian court took refuge at the Russian headquarters.

Napoleon flattered the Poles with prospects of a restoration of their independence, and received from them a contingent of 30,000 men; he also ordered a levy of 80,000 conscripts in France, to be ready by the spring of 1807. The first clash with the Russians came at Pultusk (December 26); fought in the mud of a Polish winter, it was indecisive. The Russian commander, Bennigsen, then tried a surprise attack on the scattered French winter-quarters. These manœuvres led to the battle of Eylau (February 8), in which Napoleon with 60,000 men attacked Bennigsen with 80,000 Russians and Prussians. It was a costly and indecisive victory for Napoleon; Augereau's corps panicked and was practically wiped out, and the Russians retired in good order. Both sides had incurred casualties of the order of 20,000 men. Napoleon himself described it in a letter to Josephine as a 'very stiff, very bloody' battle, and his correspondence for the next two months shows his preoccupation with the bad impression created in France and Europe by reports of the battle. He tried to counter rumours by estimating the French casualties at 2,000, and during February and March he organised with his usual skill and rapidity the reinforcements which were to bring his army to a strength greater than at the beginning of the campaign of 1806.

Meanwhile, he was saved from a serious situation by the chronic lack of co-operation among the European powers. Austria was potentially the most serious threat; she had organised an 'Army of Neutrality' of 120,000 men, but in fact she was still too shaken by Austerlitz to intervene. In March, she went as far as to offer mediation in a proposal which Napoleon, anxious to gain time, did not rebuff. He also reopened negotiations with Prussia for a separate peace. This alarmed the Tsar, who hurried to Memel, and persuaded Frederick William to confirm the alliance by the Convention of Bartenstein (April 23). But the failure of the Russians to relieve Danzig, which fell on May 24, led to mutual recriminations between the Russians and the Prussians.

The Tsar was also becoming more and more irritated and discouraged by the attitude of England. Since the death of Fox, the Whig government had become increasingly isolationist in their attitude and preoccupied with the expedition to Buenos Aires. They had declared war against Prussia over the seizure of Hanover, and relations with Prussia were not restored till the end of April 1807. English policy was distracted by a change of government in March, when the Portland government succeeded the Whigs and Canning took over the Foreign Office. When the British ambassador, Leveson-Gower, had an interview with the Tsar in June, shortly before the battle of Friedland, the Tsar showed intense irritation against England, and complained bitterly of English delay in sending forces to the Continent. "Why do you not send your militia?" he exclaimed. The Tsar also had on his hands war with Turkey and Persia, where Napoleon was stirring up trouble for him. Turkish and Persian envoys had been received at Napoleon's headquarters. Moreover, there was a strong peace-party in the Russian camp, headed by the Tsar's brother, the Grand Duke Constantine.

All these tensions and irritations help to explain how Napoleon's victory at Friedland (June 14), after a temporary reverse at Heilsberg (June 10) led to the dramatic reversal of alliances embodied in the Treaties of Tilsit. Bennigsen had allowed himself to be caught with his back to the River Alle, and his army was not only defeated, but routed and disorganised, with the loss of 25,000 men. The Tsar immediately sued for an armistice, and Napoleon wrote triumphantly to Paris that "this battle is as decisive as Austerlitz, Marengo and Jena".

When the two emperors met on a raft in the Niemen,

Alexander underwent a sort of conversion, under the spell of Napoleon's personality. He not only made peace but an alliance with France, and fervently renounced his previous policies and allies. Napoleon unfolded to Alexander a grandiose design of partnership and partition of the Continent into eastern and western spheres of influence, which would leave Russia free to deal with Sweden, Finland and Turkey, and force England to make peace and recognise the 'freedom of the seas'. By the published Treaty of Tilsit, Prussia lost her western and her Polish provinces, and recognised both a new Kingdom of Westphalia under Napoleon's youngest brother Jérôme, and a Grand Duchy of Warsaw under the King of Saxony. The French evacuation of Prussia was to be conditional on the payment of war indemnities. Russia ceded the Ionian Isles and recognised Joseph as King of Sicily. In the secret clauses, the Tsar promised to declare war on England and join the Continental blockade if England refused his mediation. In that case, Denmark, Sweden and Portugal were also to be forced to close their ports and declare war on England. Napoleon similarly promised mediation with Turkey; if it was refused, the allies were to combine to drive Turkey out of Europe, except for Constantinople and Rumelia.

Chapter Six

The Grand Empire and the Continental System

AT the end of 1807 the Napoleonic Empire stood in its most imposing form, before intervention in Spain had revealed the cracks in the structure. It is a convenient moment to consider its organisation and character.

The elaborate coronation of Napoleon in Notre Dame in December 1804, blessed by the Pope in person, marks a further stage in the reaction of the Napoleonic régime against the principles of the Revolution. It is true that he was crowned 'Emperor of the French', not King of France, and the term 'République Française' remained on the coinage until 1808; but the court ceremonial of the *ancien régime* was revived and an imperial nobility created. Many of the courtiers of Louis XVI, and the palace servants, returned to serve the new court. After the establishment of the Empire, and still more after the Austrian marriage, more and more of the old *noblesse* rallied to the new régime, and filled the court offices and the administration.

In 1804, six Grand Imperial Dignitaries (Grand Elector, Arch-Chancellor, Arch-Treasurer, etc.) were created, and the military Grand Officers, including the new Marshals of the Empire. In 1806, hereditary ducal fiefs, carved out of the Italian territories, were given to certain soldiers and civilians, e.g. Ponte-Corvo to Bernadotte, Benevento to Talleyrand. The way for the full reintroduction of hereditary nobility was paved by the elevation of Marshal Lefèbvre as Duke of Danzig in 1807, with a grant of lands within the territory of the Empire. In 1808, a regular hierarchy of titles was established—Prince, Duke, Count, Baron and Knight; their titles were to be hereditary, if they were supported by an income adequate to the rank. Napoleon had deliberately selected Lefèbvre for the first hereditary dukedom, in order to soften the blow to the principle of equality : for Lefèbvre was an old veteran of the Republic, plebeian in origin and married to a former washerwoman. Napoleon viewed the creation of an imperial nobility as an act of policy, intended to efface the prestige of the old *noblesse*, to promote a fusion of the new and the old aristocracies, and to attach everybody of importance to his person and his fortunes. But it was a policy which defeated its own purpose; the more he lavished titles and grants out of the Civil List and the profits of war, the less his followers had to look for in the way of advancement, and the less they were inclined to risk death or confiscation in further adventures. In the final débâcle of the Empire, many of the former royalists proved to be more faithful to him than his marshals and the bourgeois ex-revolutionaries.

Napoleon was obsessed with the problem of making his dynasty legitimate and permanent. It was for this purpose that he sacrificed and divorced Josephine, to whom he was genuinely attached, and married the Austrian Archduchess Marie Louise (1810), the niece of Marie Antoinette. The birth of the King of Rome (1811) gave him immense satisfaction, and he acquired the rather ridiculous habit of referring to Louis XVI as '*mon oncle*'. He put too much reliance on the marriage-tie with the Habsburgs, and was reluctant to believe that his father-in-law, the Emperor Francis, would turn against him in 1813. But he was never deceived for long into thinking that the problem was solved. His real thoughts are revealed when he said : "Conquest has made me what I am, and conquest can alone maintain me."

If the ceremonial of the imperial court insensibly tended to isolate Napoleon from public opinion, it never deluded him into confusing the trappings of power with the substance. It made no difference to his incredible powers and habits of work; though, with advancing years, his capacity for prolonged concentration declined. As First Consul, he sometimes worked for eighteen hours out of the twenty-four. His secretaries have left accounts of his normal routine at the Tuileries. Rising at 7 a.m., he read the police reports and dictated answers to his correspondence till 9 a.m., when he received his ministers and civil servants in private audience. Except on state occasions, he always wore the simple green tunic of the mounted chasseurs of his guard. He rarely spent more than a quarter of an hour at meals, and the rest of the day would be spent at his desk, at sessions of the Council of State, occasionally at more public audiences.

When he first took up residence in the Tuileries, one of his ministers remarked to him that he was taking more time over meals. "That shows already the corruption of power," replied Napoleon. He was usually in bed by 10 p.m., though on occasions he would wake in the small hours and resume work. Sometimes he would relax by strolling through the streets of Paris, disguised as a private citizen, and accompanied only by Duroc, the Grand Marshal of the Palace. Roederer once said to him that life at the Tuileries was 'melancholy'. "Yes," said Napolean, "so is greatness. . . . My mistress is power, but it is as an artist that I love power. I love it as a musician loves his violin."

Napoleon believed that power could only be exercised through fear and constant supervision. "Abroad and at home, I reign only through the fear I inspire." He told his brother Louis, King of Holland, that "a prince who, in the first year of his reign, is considered to be kind, is a prince who is mocked at in his second year". He acted on the principle that most men are actuated by low motives. At St. Helena he said : "Men must be very bad to be as bad as I think they are." He was skilful in keeping his followers in awe of himself, in playing them off against each other and maintaining a constant state of jealous rivalry for his favours. It is estimated that he dictated about 80,000 letters and orders during the fifteen years of his rule—an average of fifteen a day. One of his civil servants has written that "the Emperor exercised the miracle of his actual presence upon his servants, however far they might be away from him". Napoleon himself said : "What will they say of me when I am gone? They will say 'Ouf !' "

The desire for absolute obedience grew on him with power. One by one his more independent advisers were got rid of—Roederer, Chaptal, Talleyrand, Fouché—and replaced by second-rate men who knew only how to obey. Chaptal said of him that "he wanted valets, not counsellors". Napoleon tried to train up a younger generation of administrators through a system of appointing junior *auditeurs* to the Council of State, and even to the end of the Empire, he allowed considerable freedom of debate at the sessions at which he presided. But after Tilsit it was noted that his imperiousness and intolerance of opposition had increased. Metternich, then ambassador in Paris, observed in October 1807 : "There has recently been a total change in the methods of Napoleon : he seems to think that he has reached a point where moderation is a useless obstacle." The letters he wrote at this period show a brutal contempt for human nature, which portended disaster. As early as 1806, his Minister of Marine wrung his hands and said : "The Emperor is mad, and will destroy us all."

This was a degeneration of character, not of intellect or health. It was not till after the Moscow campaign that his physical and mental health began to be affected. Chaptal noted that "after his return from Moscow those who saw most of him noticed a great change in his physical and mental constitution". It was difficult to recognise in this ageing and corpulent man the slim, taut figure of the First Consul, with the classic, aquiline profile. Napoleon was a small man, no more than five feet six inches in height, and the British officers who saw him for the first time in 1815 found him rather ridiculous and unpleasing in appearance. They describe his walk as something 'between a swagger and a waddle'. On the other hand, they were struck by the exceptional beauty and expressiveness of the hands, the smile and the eyes.

It would be a mistake to think of Napoleon simply as an inhuman intellect and a cold-blooded tyrant. To some extent this aspect of his personality was a mask, deliberately assumed in the interests of his 'policy'. Napoleon said of himself that "there are in me two distinct men : the man of head and the man of heart". Those who knew him best in private life, his secretaries and valets, agree that he was naturally kind-hearted. Josephine said to Hortense that "people would have a better idea of him if he did not resist sentiment which he regards as weakness". He was by origin and temperament a man of the Mediterranean, of warm and violent passions and vivid imagination. If he was capable of being coarse, brutal and caddish, he could also be irresistibly gay, considerate and even poetic. Caulaincourt, his close companion for ten years, said that the "Emperor's feelings were expressed through every pore. When he chose, nobody could be more fascinating."

The charm of his manner, when, for instance, he placed the crown on Josephine's head in Notre Dame, or conversed with Goethe at Weimar, or played games with the two children of whom he was most fond, Napoleon Charles, the son of Louis and Hortense, and later his son, the King of Rome, made a deep impression on contemporaries. It is difficult to convey the characteristic spontaneity, range and pithiness of Napoleon's conversation; but he ranks high among the elect exponents of that art. He had the royal flair for being interested in people, and, except when he was bored by official audiences, quickly established a natural and easy relationship with them in conversation.

Napoleon had a keen, if capricious, sense of humour. He was once accosted by a lunatic, who announced that he was in love with the Empress. Napoleon replied: "You should choose somebody else to confide in." There was an extraordinary scene when the Dutch envoys came to Paris to offer the throne of Holland to Louis Bonaparte. Napoleon introduced them to Louis' small son, and asked him to recite the piece of French which his governess had set him. When the small boy began to recite the La Fontaine fable about the 'Frogs who ask for a King', Napoleon was unable to contain his mirth, and the whole court collapsed in uncontrolled (if tactless) laughter. In 1812, when Napoleon was returning alone with Caulaincourt from the Moscow campaign, he took it into his head to tease Caulaincourt with the prospect of being captured by the Prussians and exhibited in an iron cage in London. They drove for miles, both yelling with laughter at this absurd picture. The story of the Emperor's chicken became an epic in the imperial kitchens. One night at Vienna, before Wagram, Napoleon demanded the cold chicken which was always kept in case he wanted a late supper. When it appeared, Napoleon looked at it and complained : "Since when has a chicken been born with one leg and one wing? I see that I am expected to live off the scraps left me by my servants." The Mameluke servant who had been tempted to eat the Emperor's chicken was punished by having his ears pulled by Napoleon.

To the friends and companions of his youth, he was indulgent, familiar and attached by a bond of sentiment. Old companions-in-arms, like Lannes, Ney, Augereau, Marmont, Murat, Junot, could say what they liked to Napoleon; so could his old soldiers, his *grognards* and *vieilles moustaches*. He refused to dismiss a drunken coachman in his service, simply because he had been with him at Marengo. The tears which he shed at the death in battle of Lannes and Duroc, his old companions, were genuine and unrestrained. His command over his troops was due not only to his military genius and the prestige of victory, but to his understanding of the psychology of the private soldier and his appeal to their feelings. "The most important quality in a general is to know the character of his soldiers and to gain their confidence." Wellington admitted that the moral effect of Napoleon's presence with his army was worth 40,000 men. Napoleon played on the emotions of military glory, adventure and comradeship with unprecedented virtuosity, and his sway over the minds of his soldiers was so uncanny that it almost seemed like sorcery. Not even defeat, disaster and slaughter could break the bond between them. Even Private Wheeler of Wellington's own army records in his diary his admiration for 'Boney'.

When Napoleon boarded the *Bellerophon* in 1815, fat, middle-aged and totally defeated, he completely captivated the officers and crew within two days by the charm of his personality, to such an extent that the Admiralty were seriously alarmed. "Damn the fellow," said Admiral Lord Keith, "if he had obtained an interview with His

Royal Highness, in half an hour they would have been the best friends in England."

Chaptal goes too far when he writes (during the Restoration) that "Napoleon never had a generous feeling". These feelings were seldom allowed to conflict with his egoism, but in certain instances they clearly interfered with his policy. He may be accused of weakness and indulgence in his treatment of Fouché and Talleyrand, who constantly intrigued against him. At Erfurt in 1808, Talleyrand secretly encouraged the Tsar to stand up to Napoleon, and at the beginning of 1809, Napoleon discovered from Eugène that Talleyrand and Fouché were in secret correspondence with Murat about the succession in case of Napoleon's death in Spain. Talleyrand was disgraced but not punished. In 1810, Fouché was dismissed from the Ministry of Police for making, on his own initiative, private peace-feelers to England. "I ought to have you hanged," said Napoleon. "Sire, that is not my advice," replied Fouché. But, even in 1814 and 1815, Napoleon continued to make use of these men, whose abilities and past services he could not forget. Napoleon once aptly described Talleyrand as "a mass of filth in a silk stocking", but he also said to him. "You are a devil of a man. I cannot help telling you of my affairs or prevent myself liking you."

With his family, he was still more indulgent, to the detriment of his policy. It was several years before he could bring himself to divorce Josephine, though he was constantly being pressed to do so in order to secure the succession, and his distress over the divorce was real and intense. He showed affection and consideration for the worthless Marie Louise, her successor. Though he had many passing affairs with women, in the tradition of French monarchs, the only other woman he really loved was the angelic Marie Walewska, whom he met at Warsaw in 1807. She bore him a son, Count Walewski, Foreign Minister of Napoleon III, and was one of the few who consoled him in exile at Elba. He was devoted to his stepchildren, Eugène and Hortense Beauharnais, who repaid him with a constant loyalty and affection.

He showered wealth and position on his brothers and sisters, despite their constant intrigues, sulkings and indiscretions. Joseph, as King of Naples and then of Spain; Louis, as King of Holland, and Jérôme, as King of Westphalia, did not deserve their positions on their merits, and were a constant source of worry to Napoleon. In November 1813, Napoleon exclaimed: "I have sacrificed hundreds of thousands of men to make Joseph reign in Spain. It is one of my mistakes to think my brother necessary to assure my dynasty." Lucien, the ablest of his brothers, lived in retirement in Italy, and refused the throne of Spain, because he would not part with his wife, whom Napoleon did not consider a suitable member of the imperial family. Caroline, married to Murat, was dissatisfied with her position, first as Grand Duchess of Berg and then as Queen of Naples; so was Elisa, created Grand Duchess of Tuscany. Napoleon, exasperated with the grumblings and intrigues of his relations, once wittily complained: "From the way they talk, one would think that I had wasted our parents' estate."

Napoleon's increasing autocracy is reflected in the institutions of imperial France from 1804 onwards. The Tribunate, already reduced to impotence, was finally abolished in 1807. The Legislature became more and more insignificant, since Napoleon preferred to legislate through the Senate. On paper, the Senate had acquired important new functions in the Constitution of the Year XII, that of the Empire. Two standing committees of the Senate were set up, the 'Committee for Individual Liberty' and the 'Committee on Liberty of the Press', which could consider cases of arbitrary arrest or suppression of freedom of speech, and denounce the ministers concerned. The first committee was successful in a handful of cases; the second was debarred from considering papers and periodicals, and handled only eight cases in ten years.

The Ministry of Police, which had been suppressed in 1802, was revived in 1804, under Fouché till 1810, and then under Savary, more heavy-handed and less subtle than Fouché. The system of *'lettres de cachet'* of the *ancien régime* was openly revived by a decree of 1810, which established state prisons, and allowed detention without trial on the authority of the Privy Council. Napoleon had not only his daily police bulletin, but his 'black cabinet' for the censorship of correspondence, and his own secret agents, who kept him informed on the state of public opinion. Censorship of the press had been established by a decree of January 1800. Napoleon was firmly convinced that he could not dispense with it, but he preferred to disguise it. By 1811, there were only four papers in Paris, and one for each Department. In 1810, dissatisfied with the control of the censorship of books by the police, he set up a separate official censorship under a director-general; the following year he ordered it to be more lenient and less arbitrary and pettifogging in its methods. The theatre was also under police control, and the arts were regimented by government favours and rewards. It is only fair to add that the Napoleonic censorship was relatively mild, and was continued under the parliamentary régime of the Restoration.

Though France maintained her pre-eminence in pure science, and the portraiture of David and Gérard was notable for its realism, the state-subsidised art and literature of the Empire remained lifeless and heavy. The leaders of the new romantic movement in literature,

99

Chateaubriand and Mme de Staël, were both opponents of the Empire.

Napoleon paid much attention to education, mainly as a 'source of power', through the control of men's minds, and as a means of providing trained administrators. The Revolution had produced grandiose schemes on paper for free state education, but by 1800 primary education had sunk to a level lower than in 1789. Secondary education had made some progress with the founding of the Polytechnique in 1794, and of some hundred Central Schools. These were, however, boycotted by bourgeois families as being too irreligious. In 1802, they were reorganised, and government control was exercised through a Director of Public Instruction under the Ministry of the Interior. In 1803, the St. Cyr officers' school was founded, and the Technical School, the best trades-school in Europe at the time, was expanded. Napoleon wrote a remarkable memorandum in 1807, during his stay at Finkenstein in the interval between Eylau and Friedland, envisaging an institute of advanced historical study—a project which did not materialise.

After long discussion in the Council of State, a constitution for a 'University of France' was produced in 1808. This was not a university in the proper sense of the term, but rather a Ministry of Education, which, under its Grand Master, was to control and license all teachers. Napoleon conceived it as a sort of lay Jesuit order, to control and combat private, clerical education, which had recaptured the field of primary education and still occupied half the field of secondary education. But Napoleon made the mistake of appointing Fontanes, a clerical and crypto-royalist as Grand Master, and the university was permitted to license religious teaching bodies. Fontanes used his authority to favour religious education and purely classical studies. Primary education made little progress, but by 1813 the system of secondary education in France was the most advanced in Europe, with 6,000 students in University faculties. Napoleon had no use for the education of women; he dismissed it summarily by saying : "I do not think we need bother about the education of young girls; they cannot be better brought up than by their mothers. Marriage is their only destination."

Friendly relations with the Pope had not lasted long, since the Concordat was based on a misunderstanding on both sides. Napoleon meant to control the Pope and the bishops as his 'moral Prefects', and with his growing appetite for domination after Austerlitz and Tilsit, revived the pretentions of Charlemagne, and even the cæsaro-papism of Constantine. At St. Helena he said : "I should have controlled the religious as well as the political world, and summoned Church Councils like Constantine." Pius VII was no political prelate, but a devout priest who, although eternally grateful to Napoleon for the 'restoration of the altars', was determined to preserve the spiritual freedom of the Church and the temporal independence of the Papacy, even at the price of martyrdom. This underlying conflict of ideas might not have come to a head but for the strategic importance of Italy in Napoleon's campaigns. In October 1805, during the Austerlitz campaign, French troops, falling back from Naples on Masséna's army in Lombardy, occupied Ancona in the Papal states. The Pope sent an angry letter to Napoleon, threatening to break off diplomatic relations, which arrived at a critical moment before the battle of Austerlitz. He suspected the Pope of joining his enemies when he was in difficulties, and never forgave this insult. In January 1806, when the Bourbons had been expelled from Naples, and Eugène installed as Viceroy in Italy, he wrote to the Pope : "Your Holiness is sovereign of Rome, but I am its Emperor. My enemies must also be yours."

After Tilsit, he summoned the Pope to join the Continental blockade and close his ports to the English. When the Pope refused, he occupied the Papal states in February 1808. Finally, in 1809, during the Wagram campaign, he proclaimed the annexation of Rome to the French Empire. He wrote to Murat that "the Pope is a madman who should be shut up". The Pope was arrested in the Vatican, and imprisoned in Savona. Napoleon had unwisely forgotten what he had said to his agents before the Concordat : "Treat the Pope as if he had 200,000 men."

Despite this outrage, there was no open unrest against the Emperor in the French Church, and a majority of the French bishops supported Napoleon in his attempts to reach agreement with the Pope in his isolation in Savona, and later at Fontainebleau. Pius held firm, and countered by refusing to confirm the appointment of bishops. After Moscow, Napoleon relaxed his terms and offered Pius the Treaty of Fontainebleau in 1813, which the Pope signed and then refused to ratify. In January 1814, the Pope was allowed to return to Rome without conditions.

The consequences of the quarrel between Pope and Emperor, though serious, have often been exaggerated. It undermined Napoleon's moral position in France and Europe, and increased the fanaticism of the guerrilla opposition in Spain, Italy and the Tyrol. But most Catholics were able to recognise that this was a quarrel over temporal, and not spiritual, questions; and the origin of the religious conflict in Spain was not so much the treatment of the Pope, as Napoleon's policy of introducing the Code Napoléon, involving the suppression of the ecclesiastical endowments and monasteries.

The economic recovery of France under the Consulate was checked by the renewal of war from 1803 onwards. It is difficult to assess the financial and economic position of the Empire, since between 1803 and 1814 the French economy was mobilised for war, and sacrificed to the needs of Napoleon's 'Continental System'. The finances of the Empire remained strong, at least until 1813, thanks to the sound system of taxation and finance constructed by Gaudin under the Consulate, and to the profits of successful wars garnered by Napoleon. The *droits réunis*, established in 1804, revived the indirect taxes of the *ancien régime*—a rationalised salt-tax and taxes on liquor and tobacco. In 1811, tobacco became a state monopoly. These taxes yielded a large and increasing revenue up to the end of the Empire. The war indemnities and contributions levied by Napoleon on conquered and vassal states were paid into a separate fund, the *domaine extraordinaire*, under the personal control of the Emperor.

It was from this private war-chest, which by 1811 may have amounted to 2 milliards of francs, that Napoleon was able to make lavish grants to his generals and to subsidise the finances of the French state. The disasters of 1812 and 1813 dissipated this reserve, and taxation had to be sharply raised in 1813. Napoleon, with his fanatical hatred of credit, always refused to resort to loans; and as there was no proper system of budgeting or public accounting under the Empire, he could not have risked a failure of a public loan. At his abdication in 1814, the public debt of France was no more than 60 million francs, and the rapid recovery of the French finances under the Restoration is an indication of their comparative strength through the long strain of the war, despite a temporary financial panic in 1805 and a severe economic depression in 1810–11.

It is easy to exaggerate the drain on French manpower caused by Napoleon's wars. Before 1813, a large proportion of the heavy losses, e.g. in Spain and Russia, fell on allied and vassal states. A reasonable estimate of the number of Frenchmen conscripted between 1800 and 1814 would be 2 million out of a population of 28 million. Judged by the standards of twentieth-century wars, this was not an excessive proportion.

Napoleon paid great attention to economic questions, partly because he had been deeply impressed by their political repercussions in the anarchy of the Revolution. "I fear insurrections caused by shortage of bread," he said. "I would fear them more than a battle of 200,000 men." The workers were harshly regimented, but elaborate measures were taken to ensure the food supplies of Paris and to provide relief in times of unemployment. The Empire effectively exorcised the menace of popular insurrection provoked by hunger. Napoleon was keenly interested in the application of scientific invention to industry; in particular, it is well known that the development of beet-sugar and indigo as substitutes for colonial imports belong to the period of the Empire. If Napoleon's sweeping claim at St. Helena that he 'created French industry' cannot be admitted, it is true that he did much to foster industrial development at a time of transition to machine production.

In economics, as in naval strategy, Napoleon's sense of reality deserted him, and he acted on doctrinaire principles and prejudice. There was a strong tradition in France of mercantilism and protection inherited from Colbert, and the physiocrats of the eighteenth century stressed the importance of agriculture as the source of true wealth, as contrasted with the artificiality of commercial wealth. Napoleon had been deeply impressed by the collapse of the paper money of the Revolution, the 'assignats', and he regarded England's huge national debt as a symptom of fragility and weakness. The idea behind the Continental System—that of attacking England's credit by stifling her exports, and so draining her gold reserves—was already a commonplace in the Revolutionary wars, and Napoleon carried this idea to its logical conclusion. From 1793 onwards, the French Republic had excluded British goods, and from 1803 to 1806 Napoleon had continued and expanded this policy into a 'coast-system' reaching as far as Hanover.

After Trafalgar, direct naval action against England was indefinitely postponed; but with the collapse of Prussia in 1806, Napoleon saw the opportunity of extending his coast system into a Continental system of exclusion, through control of the Baltic coast. The Berlin Decree of November 1806, which inaugurated the Continental System, declared that "the British Isles are in a state of blockade"; all commerce with them was prohibited, and all goods belonging to, or coming from, Great Britain and her colonies were to be seized. After Tilsit, Russia and Austria adhered to the System, and Portugal and Spain were occupied the following year. Writing to his brother Louis about the Decree, Napoleon said : "I mean to conquer the sea by the land." The English government immediately retaliated by a series of Orders in Council, declaring all neutral ships which obeyed the Berlin Decree to be lawful prize, and requiring them, if they intended to avoid capture by English cruisers, to be furnished with a licence in an English port. Napoleon intensified the pressure on neutrals by the Fontainebleau and Milan Decrees (October and December 1807), which declared that neutral ships obeying the Orders in Council would be treated as English ships, and seized.

During 1808, the System appeared to exert considerable pressure on England, as shown by the drop in her exports, despite an immense development of contraband trade; but in 1809 Portugal, Spain and the Spanish colonies escaped from Napoleon's control, Turkey signed an agreement with England, and Russia was already be-

ginning to break away from the System. In 1809, the
U.S.A. lifted the embargo imposed in 1807 on belligerents
who had seized neutral ships. Moreover, Napoleon soon
began to waver in his application of the System, under
pressure from French economic interests. The ports were
ruined, industry was starved of raw materials, revenue
was falling off, and there was a glut of wheat. As early as
March 1809, he began to sell licences for export to
England, and a system of licences, with high tariffs for
colonial goods, was regularised by the St. Cloud and
Trianon Decrees of 1810. By the irony of fate, it was
Napoleon's export of wheat to England in 1810 which
eased her serious situation in 1811, when she was faced
with a crisis of over-production and unemployment, combined with a bad harvest. It is true that the Continental
System was never designed to starve Britain of food supplies (and in normal years this would have been impossible, as she depended on foreign wheat only to the extent
of one-sixth of her total consumption); but Napoleon undoubtedly missed a chance in 1811, when the cutting off
of supplies from the Continent might have created a
revolutionary situation.

Napoleon, however, regarded the Continental System
as having a double purpose—as a weapon of economic
warfare, and as a permanent protectionist policy, designed to divert the axis of European trade from Britain
to France. If, at first, he could mobilise considerable support in Europe for his attack on the 'English tyranny of
the seas', especially after the seizure of the Danish fleet at
Copenhagen in 1807, he forfeited it by his blatant subjection of the economic interests of Europe to those of
France. "My policy is France before all," he wrote to
Eugène in 1810. The line taken by Napoleonic propaganda, that Europe must unite and suffer temporary
deprivation in order to attain freedom from British com-

mercial domination, became less and less convincing when
it was clearly seen that there was little to choose between
French and British economic imperialism. Licences were
reserved for French traders, with an exception in favour
of the Americans, who resumed trade with France at the
end of 1810. This concession embroiled the United States
with Britain, but it annoyed Napoleon's Continental
allies, and particularly the Tsar.

Finally, the Fontainebleau Decree of October 1810
caused great popular unrest, with its special courts for
trying cases of contraband and orders for the public burn-
ing of English manufactured goods. As Metternich observed : "This mass of ordinances and decrees which will
ruin the position of merchants throughout the Continent
will help the English more than it harms them." Chaptal
commented on Napoleon's economic policy that he "expected industry to manœuvre like a regiment". If he had
been successful in the Russian campaign, Napoleon would
no doubt have made a supreme effort to bring Britain to
her knees by the Continental System. As it was, the
System was more or less abandoned in 1813, since Napoleon desperately needed the money to be gained from
licences.

Napoleon had not only roused the people of Europe
against the Empire by his Continental System, he had
also lost the confidence of the French middle class, the
main beneficiaries of the Revolution and the class which
had put him into power. The prolonged economic depression which hit France in 1810–11 was ascribed by
them to the Continental System; and from this period
dates their indifference to the fate of the régime and the
dynasty which was strikingly apparent in 1814. The
middle classes had shared his protectionist views and continued obstinately to hold them through the nineteenth
century, but they abandoned Napoleon when he ceased

to gain them profits. Napoleon was extremely perturbed by the Malet conspiracy in December 1812, during the retreat from Moscow. Malet, a mad Republican general, announced that Napoleon was dead and proclaimed the Republic. His *coup d'état* made some headway before he was arrested; and the significant point about the episode was the fact that none of the officials who had been deceived by Malet thought of proclaiming the accession of Napoleon II.

There was also a basic internal contradiction in the Napoleonic autocracy in France. As the middle classes had gained most in wealth and power from the Revolution and the Empire, they would sooner or later demand a share in the government. As soon as the tide of victory turned, even the servile Legislature began to demand reforms and liberties in 1813. Both in religion and in politics, the character of the constitutional monarchy of the Restoration and the July Monarchy is already taking shape under the Empire. Napoleon was well aware of this problem when he said : "All this will last my lifetime, but my son will have to govern very differently."

Chapter Seven

Spain and the Awakening of the Peoples

WITHIN a year of the Treaty of Tilsit, which appeared to set the seal on the Napoleonic Empire of the West, Napoleon became involved in the Spanish conflict, which drained the lifeblood from the Grand Army. "The Spanish ulcer destroyed me," he said afterwards. The rising of the Spanish people was hailed in England and Europe as the turn of the tide and the first example of national resistance to Napoleonic domination. The battle of Baylen (July 1808), in which two French divisions capitulated to Spanish forces, destroyed the legend of the invincibility of the French armies and encouraged Austria to take up arms again in 1809. What led Napoleon to make such a colossal mistake over Spain? The Peninsular War raises the whole question of Napoleon's attitude to national feeling in Europe and the effect of the Napoleonic domination on the emergence of national consciousness.

With the inauguration of the Continental System in 1807, it became important to Napoleon to control the coastline of the Iberian Peninsula. Moreover, he had his eye on the Spanish fleet, as an aid in rebuilding his naval strength after Trafalgar. He had always held an exaggerated view of the latent resources of Spain; he ascribed her present weakness to the incompetence and treachery of her rulers, the decadent and disreputable trio of the Bourbon King Charles IV, his Queen and their favourite,

Godoy. Lured by the prospect of conquering Portugal, Godoy had kept Spain in uneasy alliance with France since 1804; but Napoleon had become more and more irritated at the feebleness of the Spanish war effort. During the Jena campaign, Godoy had shown signs of breaking away from the alliance, and at the end of 1806 Napoleon demanded that Spain should join the Continental System and provide a Spanish corps for the occupation of Hanover. In October 1807, he sent Junot with an army to occupy Portugal, Godoy being promised the south of Portugal as a principality for himself.

As soon as a French army had crossed Spain, Napoleon was able to infiltrate more troops into strategic points. Ferdinand, Charles IV's heir, was afraid that Godoy intended to usurp the throne at his father's death, and opened negotiations with Napoleon for Godoy's overthrow. The idea thus grew in Napoleon's mind of a Spain regenerated by an efficient French administration—either by a deposition of the Bourbons or by marrying Ferdinand to a Bonaparte princess.

In March 1808, Murat was appointed to command in Spain and marched on Madrid. A revolt took place against the King and Godoy, and the King abdicated. On receipt of this news, Napoleon wrote to his brother Louis, offering him the throne of Spain, and he summoned the Spanish royal family to meet him at Bayonne. The result of this interview was that, after mutual recriminations, the King and Ferdinand both resigned their rights to the throne, and Napoleon gave the vacant crown to Joseph. Napoleon was still completely ignorant of the temper of the Spanish people. He had written to Murat in April that "if there are movements in Spain, they will resemble those we have seen in Egypt".

Murat had sent him optimistic reports of the good reception of the French in Spain (partly because he wanted the throne of Spain for himself). Until the royal family left for Bayonne, the Spaniards remained quiet, because they thought that Napoleon intended to back Ferdinand, but on May 2 the population of Madrid rose against the French, and were savagely repressed by Murat. Even then Napoleon misread the situation, and wrote to Talleyrand: "Some agitations may take place, but the good lesson which has just been given to the city of Madrid will naturally soon settle affairs. . . . The Spaniards are like other peoples, and are not a class apart; they will be happy to accept the imperial institutions." While the grandees and officials of Madrid were accepting an enlightened constitution from Napoleon at Bayonne, the provinces of Spain were flaming into spontaneous revolt. Canning hastened to give British support to the insurrectionary Juntas, and Wellington's expeditionary force to Portugal fought the battle of Vimiero (August 1808), which forced Junot to evacuate Portugal by the Convention of Cintra.

The bulk of the Spanish regular forces were easily routed at Medina del Rio Seco (July 1808), and Napoleon, underrating the possibilities of further resistance, ordered Dupont, with two divisions, to march to the south and occupy Cadiz. Here he was caught by Castanos with 30,000 regular Spanish troops supported by guerrillas, and forced to capitulate at Baylen (July 1808). Napoleon at last recognised that he had a full-scale war on his hands, and ordered the mass of the Grand Army from Germany to Spain. The Peninsular War, with its savage and demoralising reprisals, immortalised in the pictures of Goya, had begun.

Napoleon could never bring himself to cut his losses and abandon this war, partly because he persisted in thinking it was 'a war of monks', which could be stamped out by ruthless repression, and partly because he was constantly tempted by the prospect of catching the English army and destroying it in Spain. At the end of 1808 he assumed command in Spain himself, and narrowly failed to catch Moore's army in the Corunna campaign. He never appeared in Spain again, and, distrusting Joseph's competence, preferred to send orders from Paris to his disobedient and quarrelsome marshals.

The turning-point of the Peninsular War came in 1810–11. Having dealt with Austria in 1809, Napoleon appointed Masséna to command in Spain, and gave him 100,000 of his best troops to "drive the English leopard into the sea". The provincial Juntas and guerrillas had lost their first enthusiasm for the war, and, if Masséna had been successful, the conquest of Spain would have been accomplished. He was defeated by Wellington's defensive tactics at the lines of Torres Vedras, and by the jealousy of Soult, who failed to back him up from the south. Thereafter Wellington took the offensive, and by the victories of Salamanca (1812) and Vittoria (1813) drove the French out of Spain.

Napoleon was not wholly wrong in thinking that the English army was the crux of the problem in Spain. Without the military genius of Wellington and his new-model infantry (of whom a French officer said: "They are the finest infantry in Europe, but fortunately there are only a few of them"), the Spanish guerrilla resistance would ultimately have collapsed. There was always a considerable pro-French party in the Peninsular War, and if Napoleon had been able to make Joseph the independent ruler of a regenerated Spain, as he had originally intended at Bayonne, the country might have rallied to the new dynasty.

The organisers of popular resistance were the lower clergy and the monks, enraged by the prospect of the secularisation of Church property—a reform decreed by

Napoleon in December 1808. Napoleon's mistake was in thinking that there was a considerable middle class in Spain which would welcome the reforms of the French Revolution. Spain was a country of priest-ridden peasants, swayed by religious fanaticism and a traditional, unreasoning attachment to their dynasty, however degenerate. The proceedings at Bayonne were an unforgivable shock to Spanish pride, which touched off the revolt. French intervention in itself would not have produced this explosion, as is shown by the subsequent intervention in 1823, when, to the surprise of Europe, French armies marched through Spain without the slightest popular resistance. The difference was that, in 1823, the French Bourbons were intervening on behalf of the legitimate dynasty and the Church, against the minority of liberal reformers.

It is true that the insurrectionary Cortes promulgated a liberal constitution in 1812, a large part of which was copied from the French constitution of 1791; but this was mainly a propaganda effort, designed to counter the liberal reforms of Joseph's government in Madrid. It did not represent the general attitude of the nation, and the Juntas were mainly led by priests and nobles. When Ferdinand was restored to the throne in 1814, the people shouted 'Long live the absolute King' and 'Down with the Constitution'. The Spanish rising of 1808 was primarily religious, a sort of La Vendée on a large scale; it certainly has little in common with the awakening of national consciousness in the Europe of the nineteenth century, which was the work of the liberal middle class, stimulated by the principles of the French Revolution.

The Spanish affair cannot, therefore, be regarded as a typical example of national opposition to Napoleon, though it throws a good deal of light on Napoleon's attitude to national sentiment and popular movements.

Looking back to the Napoleonic period, across the developments of the nineteenth century, the historian of today is bound to be puzzled by Napoleon's disregard of these factors. It is true that at St. Helena, when he could see the trend of events, he fabricated the Napoleonic Legend, and tried to present his career as a struggle on behalf of the peoples and nationalities against the reactionary dynasties. But this was an afterthought and a travesty of the facts. The Napoleonic Empire was the negation of nationality, and never more so than in its later stages after 1810.

In his earlier policy in Italy, for example, Napoleon had appeared to foster national aspirations, by the creation of the Cisalpine Republic; then, in 1802, the Italian Republic, which in 1805 became the Kingdom of Italy. But in 1806 the Kingdom of Naples was given to Joseph, and the principalities given to various marshals were carved out of Italy.

In 1806, the duchies of Parma and Piacenza were annexed to the French Empire; in 1808 so also was Tuscany, and in 1809 the Papal states. The Illyrian Provinces taken from Austria in 1809 remained directly under the control of the Emperor through a governor-general. Finally, in 1811, the title of 'King of Rome' given to Napoleon's son, seemed to foreshadow a policy of incorporation into the Grand Empire.

In Germany, Napoleon's policy was a continuation of the policy of Richelieu and Louis XIV—to keep Germany divided by encouraging the particularism of the client kingdoms grouped in the Confederation of the Rhine. From 1806 to 1808, Napoleon inclined to a federative organisation of western Europe, placing his relatives on the thrones of vassal-kingdoms round France. But he made it clear to them that they were expected to act as agents of himself and of France. In 1810, Louis was forced to abdicate the throne of Holland, for daring to pay too much interest to the national interests of the Dutch, and Holland was annexed to the Empire. In 1810, Hanover, and in 1811, the Hanseatic towns and the Duchy of Oldenburg were similarly annexed. The creation of the Grand Duchy of Warsaw in 1807, with a constitution drawn up by Napoleon, appeared to be a step towards the restoration of Polish national independence. But Napoleon was only interested in Poland as a pawn in his strategy and diplomacy. At Tilsit, his first proposal to Alexander was that Poland should go to Russia, and Silesia to Jérôme Bonaparte; the Grand Duchy of Warsaw was a compromise solution. In 1812, at the beginning of the Russian campaign, Napoleon was to disappoint the Poles with his vague promises of independence in the future. Napoleon, in fact, never had a consistent and clear-cut plan for the organisation of his conquests : his policy shifted according to opportunity, military needs and the requirements of the Continental System. But it is also obvious that Napoleon never thought it necessary to take account of the principle of nationality.

In one aspect of his imperial policy Napoleon was consistent—the introduction of the Code Napoléon into the annexed territories and vassal states. The Code was the container in which the principles of the French Revolution were carried throughout western Europe, even as far as Illyria and Poland. In 1808, at Erfurt, Napoleon urged the kings of the Confederation to apply the Code to their states. Writing to Jérôme, King of Westphalia, and to Joseph, King of Naples, Napoleon reveals his motives. To Jérôme he says : "In Germany, as in France, Italy and Spain, people long for equality and liberalism. The benefits of the Code Napoléon, legal procedure in open court, the jury, these are the points by which your monarchy must be distinguished. . . . Your people must enjoy a

liberty, an equality unknown in the rest of Germany."
To Joseph, he writes : "You must establish the Civil Code
in your States; it will fortify your power, since by it all
entails are cancelled, and there will be no longer any great
estates apart from those you create yourself. This is the
motive which has led me to recommend a civil code and
to establish it everywhere."

Napoleon's object was thus to use the Code to buttress
his power. Why did he not realise that the principles of
the French Revolution, spread throughout Europe, would
produce the same effect as in France—a feeling of
national unity? The explanation is to be found in Napoleon's outlook as the heir of the Enlightenment and the
last of the enlightened despots of the eighteenth century.
European society at the end of the eighteenth century
had become so cosmopolitan, so dominated by French
culture, that it was possible to regard France, not as one
among many nations, but as *la grande nation*, the nucleus
of a universal state, a united Europe. The principles of
the French Revolution were, after all, of universal application; the Declaration of Rights had proclaimed the
Rights of Man, not merely of Frenchmen.

As Toynbee points out in his *Study of History*, western
Europe at the end of the eighteenth century appeared to
be in a situation rather similar to that of the Mediterranean world in the second century B.C., when the city-
state organisation gave place to the universal state of the
Roman Empire. Napoleon was tempted into thinking that
the Europe of his time was ripe for the same solution of
universal monarchy. He imagined that the sweeping away
of the obsolete institutions of the *ancien régime* through
the application of the Code would leave a flat, uniform
surface on which a universal state could be erected. As
we know from the developments of the nineteenth century, the removal of the debris of the *ancien régime* in

fact allowed the latent seeds of nationalism to thrust up and sprout.

If Napoleon fell into this error, it was an error shared by many of his contemporaries. At any rate, up to 1805 Napoleon had powerful moral and ideological forces on his side; he was 'The revolution on horseback', bringing enlightenment to Europe. (In the 1830s, Persigny, one of the founders of the Second Empire, was to be converted to the Napoleonic Legend by talking to a coachman in the Rhineland who had once seen the great Emperor passing by.) As we have seen, Spain is a special case, apart from the main stream of the development of nationalism; and even up to 1814, the emergence of a national senti- ment elsewhere in Europe in opposition to Napoleon is by no means obvious. The statesmen of the Congress of Vienna in 1814 paid no more heed than Napoleon to the principle of nationality.

The effect of the Napoleonic domination and the evolution of opinion can best be examined in the case of Italy and Germany. In Italy, the administrative unifica- tion under Napoleon, partial and inconsistent as it was, the introduction of the Code and conscription, hastened the development of the Risorgimento, signs of which had already appeared before Napoleon's first invasion of Italy. Under Napoleon, Italian troops fought well in their own units, and suffered about 80,000 casualties : their officers returned from the wars imbued with national sentiment. A few writers like Alfieri and Foscolo, forerunners of the Risorgimento, were anti-Napoleonic in feeling, because he had betrayed their hopes of national unity. From 1811 onwards, Murat inclined towards the Italian party which resented the predominance of French officials, and Napo- leon threatened him with deposition. In 1815, during the Hundred Days, Murat declared war against Austria, and issued a proclamation calling on all Italians to fight for national unity and independence. But the mass of the population was not stirred by these feelings; they passively resented the increasing weight of conscription, taxes and the Continental System, and the religious quarrel.

The origins of German nationalism can be seen in the intellectual sphere long before it affected politics. The intellectual renaissance of Germany at the end of the eighteenth century, exemplified in such great writers and thinkers as Goethe, Kant, Schiller, was at first cosmopolitan and non-political. The initial stages of the French Revolution were greeted with enthusiasm as the triumph of reason, but, except in the Rhineland, this influence remained purely intellectual and had no political repercussions. At the turn of the century, the rationalism of the Enlightenment began to give way in Germany, as in France, to the Romantic Movement in literature and thought. There was a conservative reaction and a religious revival which condemned the anarchy and atheism of the Terror, and emphasised the superiority of the unique, separate German culture to the French. But this cultural nationalism remained till 1806 confined to the intellectual sphere. Schiller in 1802 said : "The greatness of Germany consists in its culture and the character of the nation, which are independent of its political fate." And Goethe himself remained obstinately cosmopolitan in outlook, completely uninterested in the political unification of the German nation. To the end, he was an admirer of Napoleon as the embodiment of reason and enlightenment in action.

It was the humiliation of Prussia in 1806 that converted cultural nationalism into political nationalism; the younger generation of intellectuals, such as Fichte, Arndt and Schlegel began to preach patriotic resistance to Napoleon. The collapse of the Prussian government gave an opportunity for the nationalists to gain control; Frederick William was forced to appoint Hardenberg and Stein as his ministers in 1807. Hardenberg wrote in a memorandum on reform (September 1807) : "The French Revolution, of which the present wars are only a continuation, has given France, in the midst of stormy and bloody scenes, an unexpected power. The force of the new principles is such that the State which refuses to accept them will be condemned to submit or perish. . . . Democratic principles in a monarchical government—this seems to me the formula appropriate to the spirit of the times."

In practice, this policy led to the reform of the ministerial system, the abolition of serfdom and feudal tenures, municipal autonomy, and the reform of the army by the abolition of degrading punishments and the aristocratic monopoly of the officer corps. Even these moderate reforms aroused the alarm and resentment of the Prussian nobles; they feared that Stein, who was not a Prussian but a German nationalist, wanted to democratise Prussia and use her as the spearhead of a German national rising against the French. They blocked proposals for calling a Prussian representative assembly and forming a national bourgeois militia. In August 1808, Stein, excited by the news of the Spanish insurrection, was pressing for a German rising. Napoleon intercepted one of Stein's letters, and demanded his dismissal as the price of signing a convention with Prussia for evacuation and the payment of war indemnities. The King gave way and signed the Convention; Stein was dismissed (November 1808) and subsequently outlawed by Napoleon. In his bulletin announcing the capture of Burgos (November 1808), Napoleon gave a warning to Germany : "It would be a good thing if men like M. de Stein, who, lacking regular troops which were unable to resist our eagles, entertain the sublime idea of arming the masses, could see the misfortunes which ensue, and the weakness of the obstacles which this resource can offer to regular troops."

In fact, there was little popular support for a German rising, and Stein himself condemned the posturings of the patriotic anti-French society, the Tugendbund or 'League of Virtue', as the "rage of dreaming sheep". Reform was being imposed from above by a handful of far-sighted statesmen and civil servants, and, owing to the resistance of the Junker aristocrats, Stein's plans remained largely on paper. General von Yorck expressed the feelings of the Junkers when he wrote, on hearing of Stein's dismissal : "So one of these madmen has been eliminated: the rest of this brood of vipers will perish of their own poison." The one really effective reform, that of the Prussian army, was carried through by Scharnhorst and Gneisenau after Stein's dismissal. By the Convention of 1807, Prussia had undertaken to limit her army to 42,000 men, but this restriction was evaded by employing a disproportionate number of officers and passing men rapidly through the ranks for short-service training. In this way Prussia had by 1813 at least 150,000 trained men available.

When Prussia relapsed into submission to Napoleon at the end of 1808, German patriots turned to Austria for leadership. The Spanish rising and the recall of the Grand Army from Germany encouraged Austria to attempt one more throw against Napoleon. The Archduke Charles and Stadion, Chancellor since 1806, had made considerable progress in modernising the army, culminating in the formation of a reserve Landwehr in 1808. The cession of the Tyrol to Bavaria in 1806 under the Treaty of Pressburg had particularly caused resentment in Austria, and a flood of patriotic propaganda, let loose under the direction of Hormayr, whipped up enthusiasm for a war of revenge.

Napoleon had noted the Austrian war preparations in 1808, and had taken counter measures in good time. At his conference with Alexander at Erfurt (September 1808), he had assured himself of the Tsar's neutrality. By calling up 150,000 young conscripts and allied contingents, he could dispose of 300,000 men in Germany, in addition to his commitments in Spain. But it was no longer the superbly trained army of 1805 : less than one-third was composed of veterans. On the other hand, the Austrian army was more efficient and fought with more enthusiasm than in 1805. It was the combination of these factors, rather than any falling-off in Napoleon's skill, which brought him to the brink of disaster in 1809.

The series of battles, collectively known as Eckmühl, which opened the campaign in April 1809, ranks high among the examples of Napoleon's military genius. Rapidly regrouping his forces which Berthier had faultily disposed before his arrival in Germany, Napoleon had opened the way to Vienna, which he entered on May 12. A strong Austrian army was on the north bank of the Danube, and Napoleon, occupying the island of Lobau in midstream, crossed the Danube on the night of May 20. In a stiff two-day battle (Essling–Aspern), he failed to break the Austrians and had to retire to the island of Lobau.

Napoleon's defeat at Essling created an even greater sensation than his check at Eylau in 1807, but the Prussians and Russians hesitated and the English attack on Walcheren did not take place till August. Meanwhile, both sides were gathering their forces for a decisive battle. Napoleon was in control of Vienna, and could bring up reinforcements. Eugène, advancing from the Italian front, beat the Austrians at Raab (June 14) and joined Napoleon at Vienna. By July 5, when Napoleon again crossed the Danube, he had 165,000 men available against some 135,000 Austrians. In the two-day battle of Wagram, the Austrians were beaten, but not routed, with casualties of 20,000 on each side. Although the Austrians were by no means crushed, an armistice was signed on July 12, followed by the Peace of Schönbrunn (October 1809), which deprived Austria of 3½ million subjects, including the Illyrian provinces, and Salzburg, which was given to Bavaria. The Emperor Francis was disgusted with the patriots who had dragged him into an unsuccessful war without allies, and, with the appointment of Metternich in place of Stadion after Wagram, the patriots were disgraced, and their ideas, which Francis condemned as 'Jacobinism', repressed. Napoleon, on his side, had been impressed by the strength and enthusiasm of the Austrian resistance in 1809. The incident of the Austrian student, Staps, who was arrested when trying to present a petition to Napoleon, and confessed to the Emperor that he had come to assassinate him, both puzzled and dismayed him. He was forced to recognise that there was a new spirit abroad in Germany.

The nationalism manifested in the war of 1809 was of a peculiar kind, and it was Austrian, rather than German, in its appeal to the traditions of the Habsburg dynasty. The peasant risings in the Tyrol, led by Hofer, which had some of the features of the guerrilla war in Spain, were directed primarily against the Bavarian occupation. No such popular guerrilla warfare is to be found in the campaigns of 1813 in Germany itself. German national consciousness remained confined to a minority of intellectuals, and the dynastic rulers remained suspicious of its Jacobinical character. The German nationalists of the nineteenth century created a romantic legend out of the war of 1813, and christened Leipzig the 'Battle of the

Nations'. The historian must discount the legend, and recognise that the spirit of nationality, receiving its first stimulus from the Napoleonic domination, was still too feeble and obscure to exert a powerful influence on Napoleon's policy or on his downfall. Napoleon was to be defeated by his own overreaching ambition and by the dynastic rulers who, after repeated and bitter lessons, learned how to combine and to modernise their military effort.

Chapter Eight

Moscow and Leipzig

IN the winter of 1809–10, Napoleon turned over in his mind the alternative of a marriage alliance with Russia or with Austria. The failure of Josephine to produce an heir had raised doubts about Napoleon's own capacity to beget children, but one illegitimate son had been born in 1807, and Marie Walewska was about to bear him another. For the sake of his dynasty, he decided on the divorce of Josephine. At his conference with Alexander in 1808, Napoleon had broached the question of marrying the Tsar's sister, Catherine. The Tsar procrastinated, giving the excuse that he must consult the Dowager-Empress and his sister. Meanwhile, Metternich had taken the initiative in suggesting the Archduchess Marie Louise. The formalities of the divorce were completed in January 1810, and at the beginning of February 1810 Napoleon, learning that the Tsar was insisting on further delay, closed with the Austrian offer.

The failure of the marriage negotiations with Russia brought into the open the breakdown of the Tilsit alliance. Alexander had to face the fierce hostility of the Russian nobility when he returned from Tilsit. They abhorred his 'pact with the devil', and they were ruined by Russia's entry into the Continental System, which prevented them from selling their timber to England. They hated Speranski, Alexander's adviser, who was trying to reform the administration on the French model. There was even talk of another palace revolution to remove Alexander in the same way as his father, Tsar Paul. The feeling of horror and guilt about the murder of his father haunted Alexander throughout his life, and he dared not ignore the public opinion of the Russian nobility. Only one thing could have made the alliance firm and popular in Russia, and that Napoleon refused to concede—Constantinople. Reckoning that Spain was about to fall into his hands, Napoleon returned to his Mediterranean ambitions—postponed by the Continental war but never abandoned. A partition of Turkey would mean the seizure of Egypt by the British. Meanwhile, in order to keep Alexander in the enthusiastic mood of Tilsit, he suggested to him in February 1808 a fantastic project for a joint Franco-Russian expedition to India through the Caucasus, and his ambassador in St. Petersburg was authorised to discuss the fate of Turkey. In these discussions the Russian insistence on Constantinople was clearly revealed, and the talks ended in a deadlock.

By the time Napoleon had arranged a conference with Alexander at Erfurt (October 1808), Alexander's enthusiasm for the Tilsit alliance had worn off. He defended himself against the reproaches of his mother, the Dowager-Empress, who was fanatically hostile to Napoleon, by explaining that his policy was "to gain a breathing-space and, during this precious interval, build up our resources. ... Must we spoil all our work and raise suspicion of our true intentions, just because Napoleon is temporarily embarrassed?" The Erfurt conference proved to be nothing more than a carefully staged demonstration of the Tilsit accord between the two emperors. Alexander, secretly encouraged by Talleyrand, refused to put pressure on Austria to stop her war preparations; the partition of Turkey and the marriage alliance were postponed.

The Grand Duchy of Warsaw was a constant source of irritation to the Tsar, and when it was enlarged by the Galician provinces ceded by Austria in 1809, he demanded a guarantee from Napoleon that an independent Poland would not be revived. As soon as he had decided on the Austrian marriage, Napoleon refused to ratify the agreement signed by his ambassador in St. Petersburg. This rebuff was followed by Napoleon's recognition of Bernadotte as Crown Prince of Sweden, engineered by the pro-French and anti-Russian party in Sweden, and the annexation of the Duchy of Oldenburg, the heir to which was Alexander's brother-in-law. Alexander retaliated by the ukase of December 1810, which imposed a high tariff on French imports and opened the ports to neutral shipping. By this act Russia broke away from the Continental System and prepared for war.

In the spring of 1811, Napoleon was warned by his Polish allies that the Russians were massing troops on the border and planning a surprise offensive against the weak French and Polish forces in Germany. Alexander had intended to attack in 1811, but drew back, after receiving an unfavourable response to his overtures for alliance in Vienna, Berlin and Warsaw. Napoleon made up his mind, at the end of 1811, that one more 'good battle' would settle all his problems. It would convince Europe of the impossibility of further resistance, seal up the gaps in the Continental System and so bring England to her knees. It would mean nothing less than the mastery of the world.

Napoleon had not forgotten Eylau, nor did he underrate the difficulties of an invasion of Russia. When he left Paris for Poland in 1812, he told one of his counsellors that he was embarking on the "greatest and the most difficult enterprise that I have so far attempted". In the latter half of 1811, an immense mobilisation of men and supplies was set in motion. Despite the Spanish drain on the Grand Army, Napoleon could count on concentrating 600,000 men in Poland, by calling on the vassal and allied states. Prussia and Austria were forced to sign agreements to provide auxiliary forces. Caulaincourt, his ambassador in St. Petersburg, records in his Memoirs a long interview with Napoleon in June 1811, after his recall from Russia. He warned Napoleon of the difficulties of the climate, the obstinacy of the Russians and their plan to lure him into the interior. Napoleon replied : "Bah ! a battle will dispose of the fine resolutions of your friend Alexander and his fortifications of sand. He is false and feeble."

As he watched the storm gather round him, Alexander abandoned any thought of taking the offensive and determined to follow the strategy forecast by Caulaincourt. Writing to the King of Prussia at the end of May 1811, he said : "The system which has made Wellington victorious in Spain, and exhausted the French armies, is what I intend to follow—avoid pitched battles and organise long lines of communication for retreat, leading to entrenched camps." This strategy would also give him the diplomatic advantage of making Napoleon appear as the aggressor.

Napoleon had fixed June 1812 as the date for the invasion, and he spun out negotiations with Alexander to the last moment, in order to complete his preparations undisturbed. But this delay also gave time for Alexander to gain two important diplomatic and military advantages, which came as a disagreeable surprise to Napoleon. In April 1812, Bernadotte brought Sweden over to the Russian side and signed an alliance; and at the end of May 1812, the Turks signed the Peace of Bucharest. Alexander was thus relieved of anxiety about his flanks and could concentrate his forces. Even so, the Russians were greatly inferior in numbers at the beginning of the campaign. They had 160,000 men in the two armies of Barclay de Tolly and Bagration to meet the 450,000 men

127

who crossed the Niemen under Napoleon on June 25, 1812.

Napoleon hoped to repeat the pattern of his former campaigns, by enveloping the enemy forces and bringing them to a conclusive battle. But the huge superiority of numbers which Napoleon had amassed to guarantee success defeated its own object; it was too unwieldy an instrument for the Napoleonic war of movement, and it gave the Russians no option but to avoid a battle and continue retreating. Barely a third of Napoleon's army consisted of first-class French troops, and the rest were of uneven quality. Napoleon had foreseen that his troops would not be able to live off the country, but in the vast, empty spaces of Russia the army soon outstripped its supply-trains. Pillaging, indiscipline and desertion soon became rife on an unprecedented scale, and the Russian 'scorched earth' policy left little for Napoleon's army to live on. Torrential, thundery rain at the beginning of July was followed by sultry heat in August, with chronic shortage of water. The Russian rearguards fought with a courage and obstinacy astonishing even to the French veterans. All these factors combined to blunt the precision of Napoleon's manœuvres and enabled the Russians to disengage repeatedly.

The Russian retreat was, in fact, dictated by sheer necessity rather than by a planned and coherent strategy. Alexander was with the army at the beginning of the campaign, and, advised by an eccentric *emigré* Prussian, had pinned his faith to a fortified camp. This was soon seen to be a death-trap, and Alexander was persuaded to leave the army and give his generals a free hand. Barclay de Tolly, the commander-in-chief, was on bad terms with Bagration, commander of the southern army, who accused him of treason for his persistent refusal to turn and fight. Vilna was abandoned at once, and Napoleon's hopes of a decisive battle at Vitebsk were disappointed when Barclay slipped away in the night towards Smolensk; while Bagration had skilfully evaded the forces of King Jérôme and Davout and was able to join Barclay at Smolensk.

On July 28, at Vitebsk, Napoleon conferred with Berthier, Murat and Eugène, who advised him to halt the campaign, in view of the enormous wastage of troops and the impossibility of supply. Napoleon announced that he would stop at Vitebsk, and wait for a peace offer from Alexander; but two days later he changed his mind and continued the pursuit. He could not afford the blow to his prestige in Europe of an indecisive campaign. At Smolensk, on August 17, Napoleon thought that he had at last brought the Russians to bay; but after a two-day bombardment of the city, the Russians abandoned the burnt-out shell of Smolensk, and broke through the enveloping force which had been sent ahead to cut off their retreat by the Moscow road.

Napoleon again hesitated after Smolensk, impressed by the apprehensions of his staff. But he was convinced that the Russians dared not abandon Moscow without a battle, and resumed his advance on August 25. Kutusov, who had replaced Barclay as commander-in-chief after Smolensk, would have preferred to avoid a battle and let the 'scorched earth', and the Russian winter, defeat Napoleon; but his hand was forced by pressure from the court and public opinion. On September 5, Napoleon found the Russian army entrenched on the banks of the river Moskova, their centre resting on the village of Borodino. Both armies had suffered enormous wastage in the past two months. Kutusov had 120,000 men, including 10,000 militiamen from Moscow; Napoleon now had only 130,000 men available. The Russians had slightly more and heavier guns, in prepared redoubts.

Napoleon had not sufficient superiority of numbers to turn the Russian positions, and he was committed to a costly frontal assault. He attacked on September 7, and by the end of the day he had captured the Russian positions but failed to break the Russian army. He dared not throw in the Guard, his one intact reserve, in an attempt to turn the Russian defeat into a rout. The French casualties were 30,000, but the Russians had lost 58,000 men, and Kutusov had to retire behind Moscow.

When he entered the city on September 14, Napoleon expected to receive a deputation from the citizens; instead he found it deserted. That night the fires began, and raged for five days. At first Napoleon ascribed it to looting by drunken troops, but the fire-pumps had been removed, and it became clear that the city had been deliberately fired on the orders of the governor. For a month Napoleon lingered in the Kremlin, clinging to the hope of peace negotiations with Alexander. His letters and emissaries to St. Petersburg were ignored, but still Napoleon could not grasp the fact that Alexander would not, and dared not, answer. After the disasters of the Russian retreat, Alexander knew well that he would be deposed and assassinated if he negotiated with Napoleon. The nobility had recovered from their first fears that Napoleon might rouse the peasants against them by proclaiming emancipation, and all classes in Russia were now inflamed against the invader by the pillaging and devastations of the Grand Army.

Napoleon still had 100,000 men with him when he left Moscow on October 19. He had considered the possibilities of wintering in Moscow, marching on St. Petersburg or into South Russia; but there was really no alternative to a retreat to Smolensk, where at least he had a garrison and supplies. He hoped at first to avoid the devastated route through Borodino by taking a more southerly road by Kaluga, but he found the way barred to him by Kutusov and preferred to return to the northern route rather than risk another big battle. He reached Smolensk on November 8, and the first snow did not fall till November 3; but already the army was disintegrating through sheer hunger. Smolensk was a bitter disappointment; most of the stores had been eaten up by the troops on the lines of communication. After Smolensk, hardly more than the 40,000 men of the Guard remained in fighting condition.

Kutusov had been bitterly criticised by Alexander and the court for his policy of avoiding battle and letting the winter destroy the French. Now it seemed that nothing could save Napoleon from encirclement and destruction. Kutusov, with an army reduced by wastage to less than 30,000 men, was waiting at Krasnoe to bar Napoleon's retreat. Ney with the rearguard was cut off, but fought his way back to rejoin Napoleon with 800 men left out of 8,000. Two Russian forces which had been covering St. Petersburg in the north and the Austrian contingent in the south, converged on the Beresina. Minsk, Napoleon's next supply depot, was captured and the bridge over the Beresina destroyed. While Napoleon's engineers built temporary bridges farther to the north, he kept the Russian commander on the west bank inactive by a brilliant strategy of deception, and brought 60,000 men across before the Russians caught up with him and the bridges had to be burnt.

From the Beresina to Vilna (November 27 to December 9) the retreat reached the climax of disaster and horror. During this fortnight the real Russian winter set in, with frosts of thirty degrees below zero. On December 12, Berthier reported to Napoleon that "a frost of 35 degrees and the abundant snow that covers the ground brought about the disaster of the army, which no longer exists". Ney crossed the Niemen on December 14 with no more than 1,000 men fit for action. When the remnants regrouped behind the Niemen, 30,000 had survived out of the 600,000 used by Napoleon in Russia during 1812.

Napoleon had left the army on December 6; he can hardly be said to have deserted it, since it had practically ceased to exist. It was essential for him to show himself in Paris quickly in order to quell the rumours of his death which had already produced the Malet conspiracy to overthrow the régime, and to organise a new army. Napoleon's personal household had been so well organised that he suffered little personal hardship during the retreat. During the journey across Germany with Caulaincourt, he talked incessantly and optimistically. He admitted that "perhaps I made a mistake in going to Moscow, perhaps I should not have stayed there long; but there is only a step from the sublime to the ridiculous, and it is up to posterity to judge". Yet, in spite of this callous egoism, Caulaincourt insists that during the retreat there was no grumbling in the army against the Emperor.

Even when the full extent of the disaster to the Grand Army was known in Europe, it would have been rash to predict that the year 1813 would see the collapse of the Napoleonic Empire. Many Russians thought, like Kutusov, that it was no business of Russia to liberate Europe, and that the Russian army, exhausted and reduced at the end of 1812 to no more than 40,000 effectives, should halt at the frontier. Frederick William of Prussia was still oppressed by the memories of 1806, and it was only when his hand was forced by the patriotic war-party and Yorck, commander of the Prussian contingent in the 1812 campaign, went over to the Russians on his own initiative, that he signed a treaty of alliance with Alexander at Kalisch (February 28). Even so, the Russians and Prussians together could not put more than

100,000 men in the field in the spring of 1813, while Napoleon, by calling up national guards and conscripts of the class of 1813 and of 1814, had raised his striking-force in Germany to 150,000 by the middle of April.

The attitude of Austria remained equivocal : she withdrew her contingent, which had remained completely inactive in 1812, and offered mediation. Metternich, in his Memoirs written long after the death of Napoleon, tried to deceive posterity by posing as the conqueror of Napoleon and the statesman who deliberately engineered his downfall. In fact, his diplomacy in 1813 and 1814 shows that he would have preferred a negotiated peace which would leave Napoleon on the French throne or a regency of Marie Louise. Russian interference in central Europe and a Prussian leadership of Germany were as distasteful to him as the Napoleonic domination.

In the first half of 1813, therefore, Napoleon still had the chance of dealing separately with the members of the threatened new coalition. It could be done either by skilful diplomacy and timely concessions or by ruthless and rapid military force. He could probably have kept the Rhine frontier and detached Prussia and Austria from Russia if he had abandoned Germany and agreed to the dissolution of the Confederation of the Rhine. On the other hand, he could have abandoned Spain and concentrated all his forces for a decisive victory in Germany. In the event, he wavered between diplomatic and military action throughout 1813, never offering adequate peace terms and constantly reverting to a military gamble.

He was obsessed by the idea that a negotiated peace would mean the end of his régime in France. He was shaken by the Malet conspiracy and the new note of defiance in the Legislature at the beginning of 1813. As he said to Metternich at Dresden in June 1813 : "Your sovereigns born on the throne can let themselves be beaten twenty times and return to their capitals. I cannot do this because I am an upstart soldier. My domination will not survive the day when I cease to be strong, and therefore feared."

Between January and April 1813, when the main campaign opened, the French covering forces in eastern Germany, under the command of Eugène, had been pushed back to the Elbe. When Napoleon joined Eugène on April 28 with the main army, his plan was to capture Leipzig and draw the allied army into Bohemia away from its bases. Ney's corps was attacked by Blücher at Lützen, south-east of Leipzig (May 2); a general engagement developed in which the allies were forced to retreat, but Napoleon's plan for enveloping their flanks and cutting their retreat to the east miscarried. As a result of Lützen, the King of Saxony abandoned his neutrality and put his forces at the disposal of Napoleon. The allies again accepted battle at Bautzen, farther to the east (May 21); but again the turning movement from the flank, entrusted by Napoleon to Ney, was late and incomplete, allowing the allies to disengage. Napoleon's casualties in these battles were higher than those of the allies, and he found that he could not exploit them, because of his inferiority in cavalry. His young conscripts fought magnificently in battle, but were not trained for forced marches. His generals, particularly Ney, had lost their former dash and vigour. Writing to his Minister of War in September, Napoleon admitted that "the generals are suffering from war-fatigue and no longer have mobility". It is not surprising that Ney, and to some extent Napoleon himself, were feeling the reaction from the strain of 1812. In his earlier days he would never have made the fatal mistake of accepting an armistice after Bautzen. He did not realise how near to collapse the allies were, and he counted on building up his army more rapidly than his enemies.

The armistice of Pleiswitz (June 4 to August 20) was the turning-point of the campaign of 1813. Napoleon regretted it as soon as he had accepted. It did, indeed, allow him to bring his forces in Germany up to a total of 470,000, including 40,000 cavalry; but it gave time for Austria to complete her war mobilisation and pass to the side of the allies. The Prussian Landwehr was now ready to take the field, and the allies could dispose of 510,000 men, including 127,000 Austrians. The news of the battle of Vittoria (June 21) arrived during the armistice, and raised the morale of the allies.

Napoleon's chances of dividing the allies by diplomatic concessions had gone, and neither side took seriously the peace congress which sat at Prague from July 20 to August 10. Russia and Prussia had signed the treaties of Reichenbach with England (June 1813), which bound them not to make a separate peace; and Metternich had committed Austria to the allied side, if Napoleon refused his mediation. The terms proposed by Metternich as mediator were ostensibly moderate—dissolution of the Grand Duchy of Warsaw, restoration of Prussia and the Hanseatic towns, return of the Illyrian provinces to Austria. But Metternich had privately assured Russia and Prussia that these terms were put forward only as the minimum basis for preliminary peace talks; if Napoleon accepted them, their demands could be raised as the price of a definitive peace. Napoleon knew well that Metternich was setting a trap for him; if he accepted them, time would be on the side of the allies; if he refused, he would be branded in France and Europe as the eternal warmonger. When the Congress of Prague had officially closed in a deadlock, he put forward counter-proposals which accepted in substance Metternich's terms of mediation, but probably they were a mere gesture by Napoleon to show that he was not opposed to all compromise.

At the outset of the autumn campaign Napoleon's strategy was hampered by political considerations. A bold application of his strategic principles would have led him to crush the allied army of the north first, and then return with his army augmented by the garrison of Hamburg to deal with the army of Bohemia. But lack of confidence in the loyalty of his Bavarian and Saxon allies and in the mobility of his raw recruits, forced him to remain in Dresden; and he detached inadequate forces to the north, which were defeated in detail. In the south, Napoleon advanced against Blücher in Silesia, but the news that the army of Bohemia had attacked Dresden brought him back by forced marches. In a two-day battle in the suburbs of Dresden (August 26–27) Napoleon won a brilliant tactical victory, which gave him the prospect of turning the allied retreat into a rout.

The chance was missed, partly because Napoleon was exhausted and ill after five days' incessant marching and fighting; and one of the pursuing corps outran its supports, and was forced to surrender at Kulm, with the loss of 10,000 men. By the middle of September, the successive defeats of Napoleon's lieutenants had reduced the French forces by 100,000 men, and the balance of numbers had tilted irretrievably to the allied side. Moreau, who had returned from America to act as the Tsar's adviser, only to be killed at Dresden, had warned the allies to expect a defeat whenever the Emperor attacked in person, and urged them to attack his lieutenants. After the narrow escape from disaster at Dresden, this policy was pursued with increasing success; and for the next month Napoleon found himself exhausting his troops without being able to get to grips with the enemy. On October 12, he learnt that the army of Bohemia was advancing towards Leipzig, and decided to concentrate his forces for a decisive battle. He had 160,000 men in all, against converging allied forces of 320,000. The allies were still dispersed and there was a chance of defeating them in detail. But Napoleon was unable to complete his concentration till October 16, and meanwhile the Bavarians had gone over to the allies.

The first day's fighting (October 16) was indecisive, but on the 18th and 19th the Saxons deserted to the allies, and the French were forced back into the city. During the confusion of the retreat, the bridge over the Elster was prematurely blown up, and thousands were trapped in Leipzig. Napoleon recrossed the Rhine with barely 60,000 men; many thousands more were isolated and trapped in the fortresses of northern Germany.

Chapter Nine

The Campaign of France and the Abdication

THE defeat at Leipzig meant the end of the Grand Empire, and France itself now lay open to invasion. In December 1813, Napoleon had barely 50,000 effectives to defend the eastern frontier; and yet the allies, despite their overwhelming superiority of numbers, were reluctant to invade. They were held back by memories of the French national resistance of 1793, and by mutual distrust. Metternich, fearing Alexander's designs on Poland and his patronage of Bernadotte as a candidate for the French throne, insisted on making a further peace offer to Napoleon—the so-called Frankfort terms—on the basis of the 'natural frontiers' of France—the Alps, the Rhine and the Pyrenees. It was the same diplomatic manœuvre as at Prague in 1813. Metternich calculated that, if Napoleon contested these terms, French opinion would turn against him, and he took good care to let them be known in Paris. If Napoleon accepted them, he could point out that they were only preliminary bases for negotiation, and they could be whittled down in a peace conference. Neither Prussia nor England had agreed to them, and Castlereagh, on hearing of the offer, at once stipulated that Holland and Antwerp must be made independent of France.

Napoleon, yielding to the pressure of public opinion, appointed the conciliatory Caulaincourt as Foreign Minister in place of Maret, and accepted the Frankfort terms on December 2. But it was already too late : Holland had risen in revolt, and the allies had agreed on an immediate invasion of France. On December 4, before Napoleon's acceptance had been received, they issued a public Declaration of Frankfort, which evaded the promise of the natural frontiers. "The allied powers guarantee to the French empire an extent of territory unknown to France under her kings." Napoleon wrote to Caulaincourt on January 4 : "I think it doubtful whether the allies are acting in good faith, and that England wants peace. I have accepted the Frankfort basis, but probably the allies have other ideas; their propositions have only been a mask." The English government was so alarmed by the Frankfort proposals that Castlereagh was sent out to allied headquarters; and after his first meeting with the allies on January 14, Castlereagh reported to the Cabinet that: "We may now be considered as practically delivered from the embarrassment of the Frankfort proposals."

The English war aim was, in fact, the return of France to her pre-revolutionary frontiers. Castlereagh's instructions stipulated as a minimum requirement the independence of Holland and Antwerp, and a barrier against France in the Low Countries; if the war went well, he was to press for the independence of Belgium and Piedmont. Castlereagh's own opinion was that "peace with Bonaparte, whatever the terms, will never be popular, because no one will believe that he can submit to his destiny". But a restoration of the Bourbons, which was the secret hope of the English government, was carefully excluded from the official instructions, since Castlereagh wisely insisted that it must come from the French nation, and not be imposed by external interference.

Talleyrand had already foreseen this possibility, and was secretly establishing links with the Bourbon agents. Napoleon himself saw it more clearly than anybody. On the eve of joining the army for the campaign of 1814, he said: "The era of the Napoleons approaches its end and that of the Bourbons returns." When the allies finally announced, in February 1814, that their peace terms were the return of France to the pre-revolutionary frontiers, Napoleon said: "Only the Bourbons can sign such a peace." Everything still depended on the fortunes of war; only a defeat of the invasion would force the allies to moderate their terms and save his throne.

The campaign of 1814 was an incredible *tour de force*, a last brilliant flicker of Napoleon's military genius. Nobody but Napoleon would have dared attempt it with such disparity of force, and nobody else would have so nearly brought it off. "Come, Berthier," said Napoleon in January 1814, "we must repeat the campaign of Italy." And, indeed, the campaign of 1814 will stand comparison with the campaign of 1796; and this time he was working with inferior material—young, untrained, ill-armed conscripts and apathetic, war-weary generals. Wellington pronounced long afterwards that "the study of it has given me a greater idea of his genius than any other. Had he continued that system a little while longer, it is my opinion that he would have saved Paris. But he wanted patience. He did not see the necessity of adhering to a defensive warfare." This judgment does not, however, get to the heart of the matter. Napoleon's plan was to act against the flank and rear of the allied armies marching on Paris, and this plan presupposed that Paris would stand as a fortified base. Once the allies had received clear information that Paris would not resist, they could ignore Napoleon's army and march straight on the capital.

Napoleon's strategy was ruined by the political and moral breakdown of the régime. The official class had lost confidence, and was apathetic or actively hostile; and

the soul of the nation was weary. Napoleon had to pro-
rogue the Legislature after a ten-day session in December
1813, because it demanded peace and guarantees of political liberty. Nothing like the national resistance to invasion of 1793 manifested itself in 1814, apart from local
stirrings of the peasantry in the eastern Departments,
aroused by the pillaging and indiscipline of the Prussians
and the Cossacks. This failure of the national will was the
nemesis of the Napoleonic autocracy. How could he
appeal to the memories of 1793, when he had himself
crushed the revolutionary ideas, substituted his own will
for popular initiative, and asked for nothing but passive
obedience? It was in vain that Napoleon ordered the
barrel-organs of Paris to play the 'Marseillaise', and appointed commissars to rouse the Departments, in imitation
of the 'Representatives on Mission' of the Convention; his
commissars were elderly imperial officials of sixty years
of age. When his advisers talked of 1793, Napoleon himself said : "Rouse the nation, when the Revolution has
destroyed the nobles and priests, and I myself have destroyed the Revolution?"

If morale was low, the imperial administrative machine
was still intact, and a final turn of the screw provided a
certain amount of manpower and money. Taxation was
heavily increased, but no immediate yield could be expected; in the meantime, the army contractors were paid
with bills of credit, and Napoleon's private treasure, the
last bullion reserve, was used. Between January and April
1814, it sank from 75 to 10 millions. On paper there was
still an ample reserve of manpower in process of mobilisation. In October 1813, 300,000 young conscripts had been
called up, and the response was satisfactory. A further
call-up of 300,000 men from the classes of 1801–8, which
had already been thoroughly combed out, met with resistance, as it meant resort to older and married men. In

January 1814, 180,000 national guards were called for garrison duty, and 140,000 for active service in the field. Owing to resistance, delays and shortage of equipment, less than one-eighth—120,000 men—saw active service in 1814.

The allies had 300,000 men in the armies of Blücher and Schwarzenberg, but their unopposed advance into France at the beginning of January made them over-confident and gave Napoleon his opportunity. Leaving Paris on January 25, he beat Blücher at Brienne (his old school) on January 29, but on February 1 at La Rothière he found Blücher and Schwarzenberg combined, and had heavy casualties. The allies thought that Napoleon was finished, and started to march on Paris—Blücher by the valley of the Marne and Schwarzenberg by the Seine. Napoleon gave full power to Caulaincourt to conclude peace at the Congress of Chatillon, which opened on February 5. Caulaincourt reported that the allied terms were now no longer those of Frankfort, but the pre-revolutionary frontiers. On February 7, Napoleon made up his mind to accept these terms, but by the following morning he had learned of Blücher's movements, and exclaimed : "Now it is a question of other matters. I am going to beat Blücher, who is advancing by Montmirail."

At Champaubert (February 10) and Montmirail (February 11), Napoleon took Blücher's army in flank and rear, and inflicted heavy casualties. He was able to send columns of Russian prisoners to be paraded through Paris, and after the victory of Champaubert said : "If we beat Sacken tomorrow, the enemy will retire across the Rhine quicker than he crossed it, and I shall again be on the Vistula." He now turned on Schwarzenberg's army, and won the battle of Montereau (February 18). Schwarzenberg, always timid in face of Napoleon, retreated precipitately and offered an armistice. At allied headquarters, depression and mutual recrimination had replaced the over-confidence of January, and it was only Castlereagh's firmness that restored their nerve. Napoleon had offered a separate peace to the Austrians, and announced that he would only negotiate on the Frankfort terms. Castlereagh countered this manœuvre by persuading the allies to sign the alliance of Chaumont, which pledged them to make no separate peace, and to continue the war, if necessary, for twenty years. Blücher was reinforced, and resumed his advance, and the Congress of Chatillon ended on March 19 in a deadlock. On March 12, Louis XVIII was proclaimed at Bordeaux, and on March 22, the English Cabinet instructed Castlereagh that they would not accept any peace with Napoleon.

At the beginning of March, Napoleon was still hoping to crush Blücher before Schwarzenberg resumed his advance. While Blücher pushed back Marmont's force which was covering Paris, Napoleon advanced northwards from Troyes; and if the garrison commander at Soissons had not lost his nerve and capitulated prematurely, Blücher would have been caught between two fires. With the failure of this manœuvre, Napoleon was reduced to fighting two costly and indecisive battles at Craonne and Laon. His new strategic plan was to retire on Lorraine, collect his garrisons from the north, and operate against the allied line of communications while Paris held out. After a momentary success at Rheims, when he surprised a Russian corps, he decided to deliver one more blow at Schwarzenberg before retiring eastwards. Turning south to Arcis, he failed to catch Schwarzenberg with his force dispersed, as he had hoped, and on the second day of the battle of Arcis (March 20–1) had to fight with 27,000 men against 100,000. On March 22, the allies had intercepted a letter from Napoleon to Marie Louise which revealed his strategic plan for retirement to Lorraine, and dispatches from Paris which revealed the demoralisation of the capital. They decided to ignore Napoleon's diminished force, and march straight on Paris.

Napoleon's bluff had at last been called, and he had made the fatal mistake of leaving the incompetent Joseph in command of Paris, and Talleyrand at liberty to pursue his intrigues in the capital. Marmont, with Joseph's authorisation, signed a capitulation to evacuate Paris after less than two days' resistance. Napoleon, unaware of the capture of vital dispatches, could not believe that the allies would dare to march on Paris while he threatened their line of communications; and it was not till March 27 that he learned of their movements and decided to march to the relief of the capital. By then too much time had been lost, and he arrived on the outskirts of the capital, only to learn of Marmont's capitulation a few hours earlier.

Once Alexander had entered Paris, Talleyrand was in command of the political situation. Almost to the end he had hoped that Napoleon's death in battle would solve the problem of the régime. On March 27 he wrote : "If the Emperor were killed, we should have the King of Rome and the regency of his mother." He knew that there was little popular support for a Bourbon restoration, and that he himself was detested by the Bourbons. On the other hand, a regency with Napoleon still alive would be impossible, and unacceptable to the Allies. When Marie Louise and Joseph, acting on Napoleon's written instructions, left the capital at the approach of the enemy, Talleyrand decided that the cause of the regency was lost, and determined to arrange a restoration of the Bourbons. The allies issued a manifesto declaring that they would no longer treat with Napoleon, and inviting the French to prepare a new constitution. On April 1,

Talleyrand formed a provisional government, and two days later persuaded the rump of the Senate left in Paris to proclaim the deposition of Napoleon. On April 6, the Senate voted for the recall of Louis XVIII.

The story of Napoleon's abdication at Fontainebleau is told in intimate detail and sober impartiality in the memoirs of Caulaincourt, Napoleon's faithful Foreign Minister. His memoirs are, perhaps, the most valuable of the reminiscences left by Napoleon's ministers and servants—all the more so because, as Grand Master of the Horse and later Foreign Minister, he was in daily contact with Napoleon for many years, and yet he was never blind to his faults. "As for you," Napoleon said to him, "you have always told me the truth, but you don't like me." What he has to tell of those last days at Fontainebleau makes a moving and dramatic story of fallen greatness. At first Napoleon had hopes of fighting a successful battle outside Paris and continuing the war on the Loire. He still had a loyal and enthusiastic army of 50,000 men; at least this military threat could be used as a bargaining counter to save the throne for his son.

Caulaincourt saw Alexander on April 2, and reported that, while the allies were firm in their refusal to treat with Napoleon, the possibility of a Regency was not yet excluded, and Alexander had pledged himself to secure a suitable retreat for him, such as Elba. Under pressure from the Marshals, Napoleon instructed Caulaincourt to offer his abdication, on condition that his son was recognised as Napoleon II. In his second interview with Alexander, Caulaincourt was accompanied by Ney and Mac-Donald, who represented forcibly the hostility of the army to the Bourbons. Alexander was nearly won over by their arguments, but the following morning he was informed that Marmont had ordered his corps to march on to the allied lines, and demanded unconditional abdication.

Marmont's defection had removed the last card in Napoleon's hand, the loyalty of the army, and he agreed to unconditional abdication for himself and his heirs, subject to provision for his retirement. This provision, promised by Alexander on his own initiative, was reluctantly endorsed by the allies in the Treaty of Fontainebleau, which gave Napoleon the island of Elba in full sovereignty, the Duchy of Parma for the Empress, with revenues for himself and his family from the French funds. Napoleon had even suggested the alternative of retirement in England. Castlereagh reported to Lord Liverpool: "I did not feel that I could encourage the alternative which Caulaincourt assured me Bonaparte repeatedly mentioned, namely, an asylum in England."

Throughout the fortnight which elapsed from the allied entry into Paris to the signature of the Treaty of Fontainebleau, Napoleon spoke of his affairs with remarkable detachment and impartiality, as if, Caulaincourt records, "he was talking of someone else". But the betrayal by Marmont, who had been his friend since the days of Toulon, and the failure of Marie Louise to join him with his son, depressed him greatly. He took little interest in the arrangements about Elba and told Caulaincourt: "I shall not need anything; a soldier does not need much space to die in." On the night of April 12, Caulaincourt dined with him alone in the empty palace of Fontainebleau. He told Caulaincourt: "Life has become intolerable for me", and, before retiring to bed, talked at length of his reign in France. In the early hours, Caulaincourt was summoned to Napoleon's bedside, and Napoleon, confessing that he had taken poison, gave him a last message for Marie Louise and his son. "I did my best to get killed at Arcis," he said. He had now chosen poison, because he did not wish his Guards to see his face mutilated by a pistol-shot at his lying-in-state. (In any case, his valet had taken the precaution of removing the powder from his pistols.) But the poison came from the phial which Napoleon had carried in the retreat from Moscow, and had lost its power. After severe convulsions Napoleon survived, and on the following day he had recovered his equanimity. He never referred to his attempted suicide, and never again contemplated it. The authentic memoirs of Caulaincourt, the only reliable witness, did not appear till 1933; and for over a century Napoleon's attempted suicide remained an unconfirmed rumour. It would have been better for Napoleon and for Europe, if it had succeeded; but history had still to record the extraordinary sequel to an extraordinary career.

Chapter Ten

Elba and the Hundred Days

SIR NEIL CAMPBELL, who had been appointed the English Commissioner to accompany Napoleon to Elba, records his first meeting with Napoleon, when he arrived at Fontainebleau with his colleagues, the Austrian, Russian and Prussian Commissioners. "I saw before me a short, active-looking man, who was rapidly pacing the length of his apartment, like some wild animal in his cell. He was dressed in an old green uniform with gold epaulets, blue pantaloons, and red topboots, unshaven, uncombed, with the fallen particles of snuff scattered profusely upon his upper lip and breast." The conversation ranged rapidly over Wellington's campaigns, and concluded with Napoleon remarking: "Your nation is the greatest of all. I have been your greatest enemy, frankly so, but I am no longer. I have tried to raise up the French nation, but my plans have failed. It is fate."

Campbell says that on the morning of his departure from Fontainebleau, April 20, Napoleon "again referred to the separation from his wife and child, and the tears actually ran down his cheeks". Campbell also witnessed Napoleon's farewell to his Old Guard. After explaining the reasons for his abdication, Napoleon concluded: "I have sacrificed all my rights, and am ready to sacrifice my life, for the aim of my whole life has been the happiness and glory of France. . . . The happiest occupation of my life will henceforward be to tell for posterity your great deeds, and my only consolation will be to know all that France is doing for the glory of her name." With this famous scene, so congenial to the poets and artists of the Romantic Age, the Napoleonic Legend may be said to have had its birth.

On his journey to the South of France, which took a week, Napoleon was at first received with cries of 'Vive l'Empereur' in the towns at which he stopped. But in Provence it was different; Provence was strongly royalist, and was to be the scene of the savage White Terror after Waterloo and the Second Restoration. At Avignon, his carriage was surrounded by an ugly crowd, and for a few minutes there was a serious risk of his being lynched. A few miles farther on, Napoleon was forced to see himself hanged in effigy. These experiences temporarily broke Napoleon's nerve. He disguised himself in an Austrian uniform, and refused to touch the food provided at the inn that night. He was convinced that the Bourbons had sent agitators from Paris to assure his assassination. He admitted afterwards to the Austrian Commissioner : "As you know, my dear General, I showed myself at my very worst." Napoleon always had a peculiar fear and hatred of mobs, ever since the days of the Revolution; and a momentary weakness is understandable after the psychological strain of the past few weeks.

Once aboard the British frigate *Undaunted*, which was to carry him to Elba, Napoleon's spirits recovered, and he talked freely to Captain Ussher about the naval war. He developed quite a friendship with Ussher, and always spoke of him in terms of warm regard. Both Ussher and Campbell recall in their memoirs Napoleon's unfailing 'condescension and cordiality' during this voyage.

On May 4, Napoleon took possession of Elba and threw himself into the work of organising the island with the energy that once had the whole of Europe as an outlet. Bertrand, Napoleon's Grand Marshal of the Palace, had accompanied Napoleon from Fontainebleau to Elba, and the etiquette of the imperial court was carefully maintained. Campbell, who remained at Elba at Napoleon's own request, says: "I have never seen a man in any situation of life with so much personal activity and restless perseverance. . . . His thoughts seem to dwell perpetually on the operations of war." At the end of May, 700 men of the Old Guard arrived at Elba after a march through Italy; 300 more, in fact, than the number stipulated in the Treaty of Fontainebleau.

Napoleon was visited at Elba by his mother, his sister Pauline, and for a few days, in secret, by Marie Walewska, but there was no response to Napoleon's repeated appeals to Marie Louise to join him with the King of Rome. She had tamely accompanied her father back to Vienna, where Metternich appointed Count Neipperg, an elegant officer and an experienced seducer of women, to take charge of her household. Before the end of the year she was Neipperg's mistress; she bore him several children and married him after Napoleon's death. Even her grandmother, Marie Caroline, the ex-Queen of Naples and one of Napoleon's most fanatical enemies, thought her conduct abominable, and urged her to join Napoleon and defy her father. But the historic marriage policy of the Habsburgs had only too successfully subordinated human feeling to *raison d'état*.

While the British press was making bad puns about 'lack of Elba-room', and British visitors to Elba found Napoleon affable, corpulent and full of assurances that he was now 'a dead man', Napoleon was keeping an eye on the course of events in France and at the Congress of Vienna, which opened in October 1814. It is probable that, ever since the failure of his attempt at suicide at Fontainebleau, Napoleon had at the back of his mind the idea that his political career was not finished. The restored Bourbon monarchy was quickly making itself unpopular in France. The army had not lost its attachment to Napoleon, and the government proceeded to affront its officers by retiring them on half-pay and creating new posts for *emigré* nobles who had fought against their country. Chateaubriand has described in a famous passage of his memoirs, the reception given to Louis XVIII by the Imperial Guard when he entered Paris: "I suppose that such menacing and terrible expressions have never been seen on the human face. Some, wrinkling their foreheads, made their bearskins fall over their eyes to shut out the sight; some drew down the corners of their mouths in contempt and rage; others showed their teeth, through their moustaches, like tigers. When they presented arms it was with a movement of fury, and the noise of their weapons made one tremble."

Rumours that the lands of the Church and the *emigré* nobles were to be restored to their owners alarmed the peasants. By January 1815, the quarrels between the allies at Vienna had become so serious that war might break out at any moment over the distribution of the German and Polish territories.

Apart from these temptations provided by the political situation in Europe, Napoleon could not feel secure in his retirement at Elba. The Bourbon government stupidly refused to recognise the Treaty of Fontainebleau, and to pay the stipulated pensions to Napoleon and his family. Napoleon had brought from Fontainebleau considerable sums from the pay-chest of the army, but when these ran out he would be unable to maintain a tolerable existence on the revenues from the island of Elba. There were rumours, by no means unfounded, that the allies intended to remove him to the Azores, the West Indies or St. Helena. The influence of his mother and his sister Pauline was all on the side of adventure. His mother told him that she would rather he died on the battlefield than lived out an inglorious existence on Elba. The accusations of cowardice in his behaviour after the abdication were particularly galling to Napoleon. At St. Helena he admitted that "it was the talk about his fear of death and his cowardice and, generally speaking, a feeling of despair that had made him go back to France".

Campbell had warned Castlereagh: "If pecuniary difficulties press on Napoleon much longer, I think he is capable of crossing over to Piombino with his troops, or of any other eccentricity." But he was reassured by a meeting with a complacent British Under-Secretary who said to him : "When you return to Elba, you may tell Bonaparte that he is quite forgotten in Europe; no one thinks of him now." On February 16, Campbell left for a visit to Italy, and the next day Napoleon ordered his one warship, the brig *Inconstant*, to be repaired and stocked for a voyage. When Campbell returned to Elba on the 28th, he found that Napoleon and his troops had sailed two days before. Campbell had a British ship within call, but he was too late to catch up with Napoleon. There were also three French ships cruising on the route between Elba and France, and one of them actually hailed the *Inconstant*. But her captain, whether by error or connivance, accepted the assurance of the *Inconstant*'s captain that he was on a routine trip to Genoa for supplies, and that Napoleon was still at Elba. So, on March 1, Napoleon was able to land unmolested near Antibes.

Napoleon told his 'handful of braves'—less than a thousand armed men, including a few mounted Polish lancers—that "he would be in Paris without firing a shot". His understanding of the psychology of the ordinary soldier was seldom at fault, and he had been accurately informed of the state of opinion in France by a secret emissary from Maret, his former Foreign Minister, shortly before he left Elba. Nevertheless, it was an incredible gamble, with everything staked on his ascendancy over the minds of the French soldier and peasant; and even he could not have foreseen the romantic drama of the march to Paris.

Avoiding royalist Provence with its bitter memories of the year before, he set out on the alpine road to Grenoble. He was welcomed enthusiastically by the peasants of Dauphiné, but the most critical moment of the whole enterprise came just before Grenoble, which had a strong garrison and a determined royalist commander. On the other hand, he knew before he left Elba that Colonel Labedoyère, one of his faithful adherents, was in command of one of the regiments. The news of Napoleon's approach had already made the troops restive, and when the general's proclamation was read to them, stating that Napoleon had only a thousand men with him, there were shouts from the ranks: "What about us? Don't we count?" When Napoleon's small force found itself faced by an infantry battalion barring the road, Napoleon took one of the boldest decisions of his career. He ordered his men to put their muskets under their arms, and, advancing alone in his familiar grey overcoat, he shouted: "Kill your Emperor, if you wish." Ignoring all commands to fire, the battalion broke ranks, and surrounded Napoleon with shouts of 'Vive l'Empereur'.[1] It was the same when Napoleon appeared at the gates of Grenoble—the gunners refused to fire and the whole garrison went over to him. The first and most risky stage was over. "Before Grenoble I was an adventurer; at Grenoble I was a reigning prince," Napoleon said afterwards.

The news of Napoleon's landing had reached Paris on March 5, and the Comte d'Artois was sent to Lyons to command the army, with Marshal Ney as his lieutenant,

[1] This incident is confirmed in detail in the recently published memoirs of Marchand, Napoleon's valet, who was present.

who promised the King to "bring Napoleon back in an iron cage". When Artois ventured to review his troops, he was received in scowling silence, and had to fly from Lyons as Napoleon approached. From Lyons, Napoleon wrote to Ney, ordering him to join him, and assuring him : "I will receive you as I did on the morrow of the battle of the Moskowa." This was too much for Ney, and, caught up in the general surge of emotion, he announced to his troops that "the cause of the Bourbons is lost for ever". When Ney's defection was known in Paris, Louis left hurriedly for Lille on March 19, and on the evening of March 20 Napoleon was carried up the steps of the Tuileries by a wildly cheering crowd. Napoleon said afterwards that the "march from Cannes to Paris was the happiest period of his life". But the exhilaration of this personal triumph did not last long. His return had been made possible only by calling on the populace and the revolutionary forces which he had spent his life in subduing; and it was soon made clear to him that he would have to make large concessions to liberal ideas.

At Lyons he had issued a proclamation summoning the Electoral Colleges to meet at Paris, and had thus pledged himself to a reform of the Constitution. Carnot, a staunch opponent of the autocratic Empire, was made Minister of the Interior, and Benjamin Constant, a leader of the liberal opposition in the days of the Consulate, was entrusted with the drafting of an 'Additional Act to the Constitution of the Empire'. With a hereditary peerage, an elected lower house, freedom of the press and responsibility of ministers, it imitated the Charter which Louis XVIII had been forced to concede to the middle class in 1814. Napoleon himself said that it "inaugurated a constitutional monarchy". But the plebiscite which followed showed a lukewarm response from public opinion, and the ceremony of ratification at the Champ de Mai—

the last great ceremony of the Empire—was an elaborate sham. Napoleon said afterwards that he would have got rid of the Chambers at the first opportunity, and that he would never have returned from Elba if he had known how far liberal ideas had advanced. From the moment of his arrival in Paris he had been disillusioned. To the congratulations of his former ministers he replied brusquely: "Enough of compliments. They have let me come as they have let the others go."

The diplomatic situation was also a disappointment. Napoleon had assumed, when he left Elba, that the Congress was on the point of breaking up, and that the Powers, in view of their recent quarrels at the Congress, would be incapable of united action against him. But the Congress was still sitting when the news of the escape from Elba reached Vienna, and at the instance of Talleyrand the Powers at once issued a declaration of outlawry against Napoleon. This was a novel and drastic step in international law, and one from which they could not recede, even if they wished. Napoleon's pacific assurances to Britain and Austria were ignored, and the vast armies of the coalition were remobilised. His one possible ally, Murat, King of Naples, made a premature attempt to raise Italy against the Austrians in April, was defeated, and had to take refuge in the South of France.

Napoleon's best chance lay in gaining an initial victory which might dispose the war-weary allies to negotiate. He had the advantage of a mass of veteran troops, many of whom had returned from Germany and Italy since the Peace of Paris. He dared not reintroduce conscription till the beginning of June, when the class of 1815 was called up, but the regular army was rapidly expanded to 250,000 men. Of these, 120,000 would be available as a striking-force.

At the beginning of June, the only allied forces on the

scene were on the Belgian frontier—some 90,000 Belgian, Dutch, Hanoverian and English under Wellington, and some 120,000 Prussians under Blücher. Napoleon's plan was to surprise them while they were still strung along the frontier, and beat them separately. His strategical concentration was as brilliantly conceived and executed as ever. By June 14, he had brought 120,000 men to the frontier at Charleroi before Wellington and Blücher were even aware that he was taking the offensive. On the 15th, the French drove back an isolated Prussian corps; Blücher concentrated his forces, and was able to mass 90,000 men at Ligny on the 16th. Wellington was slow to act, and on the 16th not more than a third of his force was able to reach Quatre Bras, covering the direct road to Brussels. Napoleon instructed Ney to contain Wellington's forces at Quatre Bras, and to spare every man he could for an attack on the right flank of the Prussians, while he himself attacked the Prussian centre.

Ney unaccountably delayed action until midday, giving time for Wellington's reserves to come up from Brussels. Napoleon found the Prussians in greater strength than he had expected, and did not begin his attack till the afternoon. The French reserve corps under d'Erlon was approaching Quatre Bras when an order from Napoleon arrived, diverting it on to the Prussian right. Unfortunately d'Erlon acted on a later order from Ney, summoning him to help at Quatre Bras, and failed to arrive in time at either battlefield. Napoleon defeated and drove back the Prussians, but the enveloping movement which could have turned the defeat into a rout had miscarried.

On the morning of the 17th, Napoleon ordered Grouchy with 33,000 men to pursue the Prussians but to keep in touch through his left flank, while he himself joined Ney to deal with Wellington. But there was a fatal delay in beginning these movements, partly because of

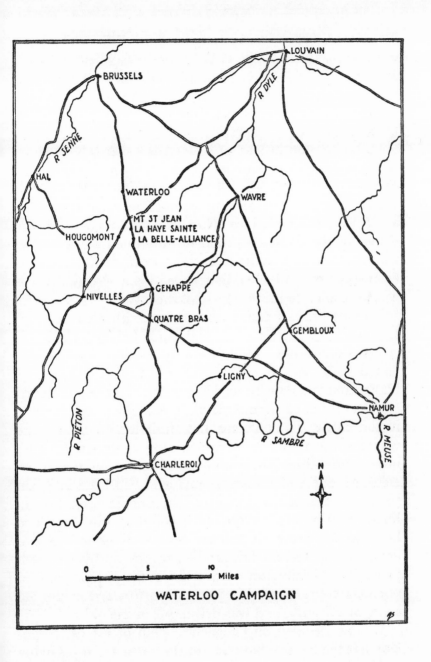

WATERLOO CAMPAIGN

157

Napoleon's fatigue and partly because of the exhaustion of the troops after the fierce battle of the day before. Napoleon lost the chance of beating Wellington on the 17th, who was able to retire to Mont St. Jean, and Grouchy's cavalry lost touch with the Prussians. Blücher had taken the crucial decision to retire northwards and keep touch with Wellington instead of eastwards towards his lines of communication, as Napoleon confidently assumed. Thus, on June 18, Napoleon with 74,000 men faced Wellington with 67,000 men at Mont St. Jean. The stage was set for a decisive battle, since Napoleon assumed that the Prussians were out of action or contained by Grouchy, whereas Wellington had received during the night an assurance from Blücher that at least one Prussian corps would reach him in the course of the day.

Wellington had chosen his ground with his usual tactical skill—the crest of a slight hill behind which his reserves could mass unharassed by artillery fire. But his mixed army contained only 24,000 British troops, and he had made a dangerous detachment of 17,000 to guard against an attack from his right flank, which took no part in the battle. To Napoleon the affair looked simple : he would waste no time in manoeuvring against the flanks, but smash through Wellington's centre with massed columns. Some of his lieutenants who had been in Spain reminded him of the strength of the English fire-power in line-formation against attacking columns, but Napoleon brushed this aside. "I tell you that Wellington is a bad general, that the English are bad troops, and it will be a picnic." As Wellington said afterwards : "Napoleon did not manoeuvre at all. He just moved forward in the old style, in columns, and was driven off in the old style."

Having decided on his general plan of attack, Napoleon left the tactical handling of the battle to Ney. Owing to the heavy rain of the past twenty-four hours, mud delayed the main attack till 1.30 p.m. when four densely massed columns were thrown back with heavy loss. By this time the position was critical, as the Prussian columns were approaching the French right flank, and Napoleon had received news from Grouchy that he was held up by a Prussian corps at Wavre, thirteen miles away. Napoleon could have broken off the battle at this point, but the campaign would have been lost; and he preferred to gamble on a victory before the Prussians could intervene decisively. Detaching 10,000 men to contain the Prussians, he ordered Ney to resume the attack at 3.30 p.m. Ney made the mistake of sending in the cavalry alone against the unbroken British squares. Napoleon exclaimed : "There is Ney hazarding the battle which was almost won; but we must support him now, it is our only chance." In fact, Napoleon missed the last chance when, at 6.30 p.m., the French infantry carried the fortified position of La Haye Sainte, and caused a breach in the British centre. He refused to release the last reserves of the Guard to Ney at this moment, and when he decided on a last attack with the Guard after 7 p.m., Wellington had been given time to repair the gaps in his line. When this last assault by the Guard failed, and Wellington sent in his cavalry, the French army broke in panic-stricken rout. Barely 8,000 men escaped in fighting-order, but Grouchy retired on Namur with his 30,000 men intact.

The campaign which had started so brilliantly was ruined by serious blunders in execution—the confusion of orders to d'Erlon's corps on the day of Quatre Bras and Ligny, the fatal delay in following up the Prussians after Ligny, Napoleon's serious underestimate of Wellington and the British infantry on the day of Waterloo. It seems clear from the evidence of Napoleon's valet, Marchand, who was with him throughout the campaign, that Napoleon was no longer equal to the physical and mental exertion required by the Napoleonic type of warfare, and he badly missed Berthier, his invaluable chief of staff. Napoleon said afterwards : "I had no longer within me the feeling of certain success." Nor was Ney the man he had been; he had never recovered from the exertions of 1812, and was oppressed by a feeling of guilt at his change of allegiance. Grouchy was a good cavalry leader but had no experience of an independent command. He was at a loss without precise orders, and showed an incredible lack of grasp of the Napoleonic principles of strategy, when he failed to make sure, at all costs, that he would not be too far away to join up with Napoleon or bar the way to the Prussians on the day of Waterloo.

Remembering his mistake in 1814, Napoleon hastened back to Paris to control the politicians. He wrote to his brother Joseph on the day after Waterloo that all was not lost; he could still collect 150,000 men, arm the people. At a meeting of the Council on the day after his return to Paris, he spoke eloquently of his plans for continuing the fight. Fouché, reinstated in his old position as Minister of Police, said after the meeting : "That devil of a fellow gave me a fright this morning. Listening to him I thought we were going to begin all over again. Fortunately we are not going to begin all over again."

Like Talleyrand in 1814, Fouché had arranged the obsequies of the Empire and the recall of the Bourbons. The liberal majority in the Chamber, organised by Fouché, forestalled Napoleon by declaring that any attempt to dissolve the Chamber was treason to the nation. Napoleon could still have dissolved it by force, and resorted to a military dictatorship, since the army and the people of Paris were still his enthusiastic followers. But, as in 1814, he recoiled from the idea of "beginning the Revolution over again", and on June 22 signed an act of abdication in favour of his son. The Chamber ignored the proposal for setting up a Regency for Napoleon II, and simply nominated a provisional government. Napoleon retired to Malmaison, and, after a last offer to lead the army as a general, was persuaded to move to Rochefort on June 29, as the Prussians approached Paris. On July 8, Louis XVIII re-entered Paris 'in the baggage-train of the allies'.

Chapter Eleven

St. Helena and the Napoleonic Legend

IT may be argued that Napoleon's career was finished at Waterloo and that little more remains to be said. He was transported to St. Helena, and died there a prisoner in 1821. But it was impossible for Napoleon to relinquish a political role as long as he was alive; he was merely exchanging the sword for the pen as a political weapon. The writings which emanated from St. Helena laid the foundations of the Second Empire. Moreover, for the historian the story of St. Helena is of incomparable interest for the light which it throws on Napoleon's character. The English who came into contact with him on the voyage there and on the island saw him stripped of power and with eyes which were not dazzled by hero-worship.

There were two French frigates lying near Rochefort, and the French government had asked the British government for safe conduct for Napoleon to the U.S.A. This was refused, and Captain Maitland of the *Bellerophon*, which was blockading that part of the coast, was ordered to intercept and bring Napoleon to the nearest British port. Various plans for evading the blockade were proposed to Napoleon, but he finally discarded them and resolved to give himself up voluntarily to the *Bellerophon*. The idea of an 'asylum in England' had already occurred to him in 1814, and it had been strengthened by the favourable impression he had formed of the English he had met at Elba. "There is always some danger in trusting to one's enemies," he said, "but it is better to risk reliance on their sense of honour than be in their hands as a prisoner by law." When Napoleon's emissaries met Maitland, he made it perfectly clear that he was not in a position to give any pledges about the treatment Napoleon would receive from the English government, but he did not discourage the idea that Napoleon would be allowed to live in England. Before boarding the *Bellerophon*, Napoleon wrote the famous letter to the Prince Regent which is now in the Royal Library at Windsor. "I come, like Themistocles, to claim a seat by the hearth of the British people. I put myself under the protection of the law which I claim from your Royal Highness as the most powerful, the most constant and the most generous of my enemies."

Napoleon knew perfectly well the risks he was running in the surrender, but he was banking on the generosity of the British people and the fascination of his personality. Maitland records that "from the time of his coming on board ship, his conduct was invariably that of a gentleman". On the *Bellerophon* he was treated as a royal personage. Maitland explains that : "It may appear surprising that a possibility could exist of a British officer being prejudiced in favour of one who had caused so many calamities to his country; but to such an extent did he possess the power of pleasing, that there are few people who could have sat at the same table with him for nearly a month, as I did, without feeling a sensation of pity, allied perhaps to regret, that a man possessed of so many fascinating qualities, and who had held so high a station in life, should be reduced to the situation in which I saw him." When Napoleon left the *Bellerophon*, Maitland asked his servant what the ship's company thought of Napoleon. He replied : "I heard several of them conversing this morning and one observed, 'Well, they may abuse that man as much as they like, but if the people of England knew him as well as we do, they would not hurt a hair of his head.' They all agreed." While the *Bellerophon* lay first at Torbay and then at Plymouth, she was besieged by hordes of sightseers in boats, anxious to catch a glimpse of 'Boney'. Lieutenant Bowerbank of the *Bellerophon* recalls that : "I was surprised at not hearing a disrespectful or abusive word escape from any one. On the contrary, the spectators generally took off their hats when he bowed." If Napoleon had once landed on English soil, there would have been a fair chance of his conquering the hearts of the English people.

It was a bitter moment, therefore, for Napoleon when Admiral Lord Keith announced to him the decision of the English government. He was to be sent to St. Helena, and treated, no longer as ex-Emperor, but as a general on retired pay. Napoleon protested in writing : "I am not the prisoner, but the guest of England. If the government, in ordering the captain of the *Bellerophon* to receive me, as well as my suite, desired only to set a trap, it has forfeited its honour and sullied its flag." This charge of perfidy will not stand examination; Napoleon knew perfectly well that he had surrendered at discretion as a prisoner-of-war. Nor can the choice of St. Helena be questioned; it had a reasonably healthy climate, and could be effectively guarded without close restrictions on Napoleon's liberty. To keep him in England was an impossibility, since, as Liverpool wrote to Castlereagh, "you know enough of the feelings of people in this country not to doubt he would become an object of curiosity immediately, and possibly of compassion, in the course of a few months." The English Whigs and Radicals professed admiration for Napoleon, and the Tory government were frightened not only of Napoleon but of Jacobinism, of which he was still the symbol.

The Allies had agreed with the St. Helena decision, and would certainly have been suspicious of English designs if he had been kept in England. The real charge against the English government is the lack of magnanimity and imagination, markedly different from the instinctive reaction of the English people, with which they carried out their unpleasant and unprecedented task. The refusal to recognise Napoleon's title as ex-Emperor was an unnecessary and petty insult, and the management of Napoleon's internment at St. Helena was entrusted to the wrong hands.

When Napoleon was transferred from the *Bellerophon* to the *Northumberland* for the three months' voyage to St. Helena, he was allowed to bring with him a considerable suite—Bertrand, two court chamberlains, Montholon and Lascases (both of them ex-royalist nobles of the *ancien régime*), General Gourgaud and twelve servants. Bertrand and Montholon brought their wives and young children, and Lascases his young son. Napoleon adapted himself with good humour to the crowded quarters of the *Northumberland* and to his new status as a retired general and prisoner-of-war; he started to dictate his memoirs, and spent the evenings playing cards with the English officers.

The six years of Napoleon's life at St. Helena contain elements of high tragedy, pathos, triviality and farce inextricably mixed. For the first month, while his permanent home, Longwood, was being prepared for him, Napoleon occupied a small pavilion in the garden of the country-house of Mr. Balcombe, an English merchant. Separated from his suite, he amused himself by making friends with the Balcombe daughters—two wild English hoydens, aged fifteen and thirteen. Betsy, the younger,

could talk French, and she treated Napoleon as a favourite uncle and playmate. Napoleon always enjoyed the
company of children, and he entered into her wild pranks
with gaiety and good humour. She made him play whist
(at which he invariably cheated) and blind-man's-buff;
Napoleon helped her with her French lessons. When she
told him about her friend who was terrified of meeting
the 'Corsican ogre', and introduced her, Napoleon obligingly made a horrible face and growled at her. Betsy was
shut up in the cellar by her father for showing Napoleon
a new toy which had arrived from England, depicting
'Boney' climbing up a ladder and then falling headlong
to St. Helena. Napoleon consoled her with sweets during
her imprisonment. Lascases and Gourgaud were outraged
by Betsy's casual behaviour towards the Emperor. But
Napoleon was enjoying his first holiday for a long time.
"I thought I was at a masked ball," he said, "listening to
the absurd questions of these girls." Betsy has her niche
in history for introducing this interlude of rustic farce
into Napoleon's life. The Balcombe family remained
staunch friends of Napoleon till they left in 1820, and
Napoleon gave Betsy a lock of his hair. She thought then
that he had the look of a dying man. Shortly before her
death she was presented by Napoleon III with an estate
in Algeria, in memory of her friendship with his uncle.

The move to Longwood and the arrival of Sir Hudson
Lowe as Governor embittered the remainder of Napoleon's life. It is true that Napoleon was determined to
exploit every grievance, and make himself into a 'martyr'.
He told his followers from the start that it was their duty
to complain. He boasted to Admiral Malcolm that: "I
have worn the imperial crown of France, the iron crown
of Italy. England has now given me a greater and more
glorious crown than either of them—for it is that worn
by the Saviour of the World—a crown of thorns." Some-

times he thought that "from the point of view of history, I should have died at Moscow, Dresden or Waterloo". For the first year or two, he still hoped that political developments in Europe might bring him back from St. Helena, but he never seriously thought of escape. Napoleon's mother, backed by Pope Pius VII, whom he had persecuted, appealed to the sovereigns assembled at the Congress of Aix-la-Chapelle in 1818, but the Congress merely reaffirmed the conditions of Napoleon's detention. After that Napoleon gave up all hope of return. At Longwood, he insisted on being treated as Emperor in his own house, and refused all invitations to English houses, because his imperial dignity was not recognised. For him, this was a matter of policy—the preservation of the memory and the claims of his dynasty on behalf of his son. He complained about the unhealthiness of Longwood and the narrow limits beyond which he could not ride without an English escort. (No less than 3,000 troops held guard round Longwood, and a squadron of warships was employed in patrolling the island.)

Lowe was an unfortunate choice for a situation demanding great tact. He was not a gentleman of the same stamp as the naval officers with whom Napoleon had personally been on friendly terms; he was morbidly suspicious, and terrified of displeasing the ministers in London. He organised an odious system of espionage in the island, and even Admiral Malcolm, the naval commander, ended by quarrelling with him. Wellington, under whom he had served, said "he was a damned fool". His impertinent and shifty manner, and his petty annoyances, infuriated Napoleon; he even confiscated a book sent to Napoleon by an English admirer, because it was dedicated to 'Imperatori Napoleoni'. After 1816, Napoleon refused to see him again. "He makes me too angry and I forget myself."

A state of cold war now existed between Longwood and the governor. When Lowe ordered the running costs of Longwood to be cut down, Napoleon sent his silver plate to be sold in the town, and shamed Lowe into rescinding the order. Napoleon had £250,000 in British funds, which had been transferred there on his behalf by a French banker after Waterloo, but he did not wish to disclose this to the British Government. When the restrictions on Napoleon's movements were tightened up, he gave up riding, and this led to a rapid deterioration in his health. Napoleon offered to settle the dispute over his name by adopting an incognito title, but the Ministry in London quashed the idea. But for these squalid and unnecessary disputes, Napoleon could have led a much more tolerable and healthy existence, since both Malcolm and the Russian Commissioner on the island were convinced that it was perfectly safe to guard the beaches, and leave Napoleon the full liberty of the island.

Napoleon had also to put up with the jealousies and quarrels of his followers, whose nerves were affected by the boredom and strain of the life of a prison-camp. None of them, except Bertrand, were old friends of long standing, and in despair he once said to Gourgaud : "If I had known what it would be like, I should have brought nothing but servants." But on the whole he showed more patience and equanimity than his followers, whose exile was not permanent. Gourgaud was a temperamental young man, jealously devoted to Napoleon, who treated him like a wayward son. There was a terrible scene when Napoleon accused Gourgaud of perpetually sulking, and said : "Do you not think that when I wake in the night I don't have bad moments, when I recall what I was and what I am now?" Gourgaud was in tears, and Napoleon consoled him by pointing out that : "If I was not fond of you, I would not trouble to talk to you like this." Gourgaud's behaviour finally became impossible, and Napoleon approved of his departure for Europe in 1817; Lascases had already been deported at the end of 1816 for trying to smuggle out correspondence.

Gourgaud records in his Journal another painful moment, when the conversation turned to statistics. Napoleon took down the Almanack of the Empire, and, looking through the pages, murmured : "It was a fine Empire. I had 83 millions of men to govern, more than half the population of Europe." Napoleon tried to sing in order to hide his emotion. But life at Longwood was not all gloom. Warden, the surgeon of the *Northumberland*, called at Longwood, and went for a drive with Napoleon and his suite. Napoleon kept the whole company in fits of laughter by talking English and deliberately getting all the words wrong.

In 1818, Napoleon had an attack of the liver disease which was prevalent in the island, and his health then began to break down. By the end of 1819, disease of the stomach made him unable to eat, and after four months of painful illness he died on May 5, 1821. The last words he uttered on his death-bed were "at the head of the army" and the name of his son. Almost to the end, Lowe thought that his illness was feigned. The official British diagnosis of the cause of his death was cancer of the stomach of long standing. The French view was that it was due to disease of the liver, contracted in the climate of St. Helena. The real cause, so far as it can be determined, was a gastric ulcer, aggravated by lack of exercise and incompetent medical treatment. In different circumstances, mental and physical, he might have lived considerably longer.

Napoleon was fairly well supplied with books and periodicals at St. Helena, and spent much of his time in dictating his 'memoirs', which were first published in

1823. They are a disappointing monument to his genius: mostly accounts of his earlier campaigns, written in a dull, impersonal style, altogether lacking in the characteristic tone of his bulletins, proclamations and conversations. Only in his will, dictated a month before his death, does he recapture his power over words. "I desire that my ashes repose on the banks of the Seine, in the midst of the French people whom I have loved so dearly. . . . I die prematurely, murdered by the English oligarchy and its hired assassin. The English people will not be slow in avenging me. . . . I urge my son never to forget that he was born a French prince, and never to lend himself to being an instrument in the hands of the triumvirs who are oppressing the peoples of Europe."

The records of Napoleon's conversations kept by his companions at St. Helena were much more valuable and influential than his formal 'memoirs'. Napoleon encouraged his followers to write down what he said, and told them that they would make their fortunes by doing so. Gourgaud, Bertrand, and Marchand, the valet, kept journals which were not intended for publication, and have only appeared in this century. These give a comparatively true and unvarnished picture of Napoleon at St. Helena. Lascases, Montholon and O'Meara[1] published their accounts immediately after Napoleon's death; they sold in enormous numbers, and launched the Napoleonic Legend. Through the distortions of their different styles, the authentic voice of Napoleon can be heard, deliberately impressing on the world what he wanted people to believe about his career and his policy.

Attuning himself to the trend of politics since 1814, Napoleon refashioned his career in the interests of his son

---

[1] O'Meara was the British naval surgeon who accompanied Napoleon to St. Helena as his physician, quarrelled with Lowe in 1818, and returned to England a violent partisan of Napoleon.

and of his own reputation as an historical figure. The Powers which had overthrown him in 1814 and 1815 were now the Holy Alliance, the declared enemies of liberalism and nationalism, and it was not difficult for Napoleon to show himself as the champion of these forces. His reign had been based, not only on equality but on liberty, and here he could point to the liberal constitution of the Hundred Days. His autocracy was only intended for the temporary emergency. "If I had won in 1812, my constitutional reign would have begun." He was "the natural mediator in the struggle of the past against the Revolution"—the synthesis of monarchy and liberalism. He always wanted peace, but the dynasties of the *ancien régime* would not allow it. If he had been given time, he would have fulfilled national aspirations. "There are in Europe more than thirty million French, fifteen million Spanish, fifteen million Italians and thirty million Germans. I would have wished to make each of these peoples a single united body." He would have restored Polish independence; Germany would demand more time, and it was necessary first to "simplify their complications". His policy in Italy was intended "to supervise, guarantee and advance the national education of the Italians". He admitted his error in offending the pride of the Spanish people by dethroning the Bourbon dynasty, but it was done with the best intentions of regenerating Spain. "Europe thus divided into nationalities freely formed and free internally, peace between states would become easier; the United States of Europe would become a possibility."

All this, with its suppression of awkward facts and its skilful twisting of Napoleon's real policy, could be made plausible to the generation growing up after Waterloo, which had not seen the battlefields of the Empire. It was not difficult, also, for the author of the Concordat to pose as the champion of Catholicism. In his will, he wrote : "I die in the Catholic, Apostolic and Roman faith in which I was born more than fifty years ago." He died attended by the full rites of the Church. Lascases and Montholon represent Napoleon at St. Helena as turning to a belief in the Christian religion; but Bertrand thought that the declaration in his will was 'policy'. A month before his death, he said to Bertrand : "I am glad I have no religion. It is a great consolation; I have no imaginary fears, no fear of the future." Bertrand and Gourgaud record conversations in which Napoleon argued from an agnostic or materialist point of view. He was too intelligent to be a dogmatic atheist, but he could not himself believe, though he thought it proper that "one should die in the faith of one's fathers". It is probable, therefore, that he remained an agnostic, but one who was profoundly convinced of the social importance of religion. "A religion is necessary," he said to Gourgaud, "to cement the union of men in society." On the whole, he thought that Mohammedanism was a more effective religion than Christianity.

Napoleon had his posthumous victory in the creation of the Legend. His son, the King of Rome, died as an Austrian Archduke, the Duke of Reichstadt, in 1832; but in 1840 the government of Louis Philippe brought back Napoleon's body from St. Helena, and interred it with great pomp in the Invalides. Bertrand, Gourgaud and Marchand helped to bring back the coffin. In 1852, the Empire was restored in the person of Napoleon's nephew, Napoleon III. In 1855, Queen Victoria stood with Napoleon III in the Invalides and ordered her small son, the future Edward VII, to "kneel down before the tomb of the great Napoleon".

Despite the cynical remark of a French general in the First World War that "Napoleon was not a great general

—he only had to fight coalitions", it can safely be said that Napoleon was the greatest man of action whose life is known to historians in intimate detail. Talleyrand, his old friend and enemy, said after his death that "his genius was unbelievable. It is the most astonishing career that has been witnessed for the last thousand years. He was certainly the most extraordinary man I ever saw, and in my opinion the most extraordinary man that has lived for many centuries." It is tempting to compare him with the dictators of a later age, such as Hitler, but the comparison is really misleading. Napoleon did not owe his rise to power to the arts of a demagogue or a party-manager (though he was no mean exponent of the art of propaganda), but to his transcendent ability as a military leader and as a ruler. Such a combination of qualities can hardly be paralleled in the modern world; and he is more akin to the world conquerors of ancient times, who were his inspiration.

The 'great men' of history cannot, of course, achieve much unless circumstances favour them, and Napoleon's career is a perfect example of the interaction of the individual and the mass. Napoleon remarked at St. Helena: "A man is only a man. His power is nothing if circumstances are not favourable. Opinion is all-important. If I had not appeared someone else would have done the same thing. I consider that I count for no more than half in the battles which I have won. The general's name is hardly worth mentioning, for the fact is that it is the army which wins the battle." In a sense, Napoleon merely exploited the energies and instruments created by the French Revolution; when they were exhausted, he was swept away. But it would be impossible to deny that without his personality the course of events would have been different.

It is significant that time has not confirmed his title of

'Napoleon the Great'. Talleyrand, who possessed the sense of moderation and balance which Napoleon lacked, said : "What a tragedy that he gave his name to adventures instead of to the ages." Despite his enormous influence on the development of France and Europe, Napoleon failed to found a durable monument to his fame. There is considerable substance in Napoleon's claim at St. Helena that his dynasty alone could reconcile the Revolution with the past. The curse of France since 1815 has been the instability of her politics, and the deep rift in French society, created by the Revolution and aggravated by the collapse of monarchical and aristocratic institutions. The Bourbon dynasty was too wedded to clericalism and the *ancien régime*; the Orleanist dynasty lacked tradition and glamour. By 1810 Napoleon had practically achieved the fusion of monarchy and the Revolution in France. And it is arguable that a longer period of Napoleonic rule might have been a benefit to Europe. The liberal and national movements of the nineteenth century might have developed more fruitfully if the middle class in Europe had had a concrete experience of European unity and a thorough training in government through the Napoleonic administration.

Napoleon's work was ruined by his pursuit of the impossible dream of world dominion, beyond the capacity of France and of Napoleon himself. War undoubtedly fascinated and intoxicated Napoleon's mind as the supreme form of gambling. He once said "that the greatest immorality is to do a job for which one is not qualified"; and his mastery of the art of war tempted him to rely on it more and more. At the beginning of 1814 he made a remarkable statement : "I am not afraid to admit that I have waged war too much. I wanted to assure for France the mastery of the world." One of the poets of the Romantic Age after Waterloo said of him :

"A streak of divine folly runs through all his work." He understood the romantic ambition for unlimited personal glory which is the driving force in Napoleon's career. Yet even as a romantic hero, he falls short of Nelson, because his career lacks the grand simplicity and poetry of a life dedicated to a single cause greater than himself.

Historians of Napoleon are apt either to be fascinated into adulation by his personality or repelled by the spectacle of the millions of lives sacrificed to his ambition. Fortunately it is not the duty of historians to usurp the function of the Deity and to pass judgment on a man's life (though they are often tempted to do so), but to tell the truth. The Greeks would have understood Napoleon's story as a simple case of Hubris followed by Nemesis; and perhaps it is better to leave it at that. As a man, Napoleon was not particularly cruel, wicked or vindictive; his sins were on the heroic scale—the sins of pride. Even his enemies admitted that he waged war according to the accepted standards of his age.

It is legitimate to admire his genius while deploring the ends to which it was put. Perhaps the greatest tribute that can be paid to him is the fact that his personality remains, with all its obvious faults of character and judgment, potentially greater and more complex than his achievements. Chateaubriand hardly exaggerates when he sums up Napoleon as "the mightiest breath of life which ever animated human clay".

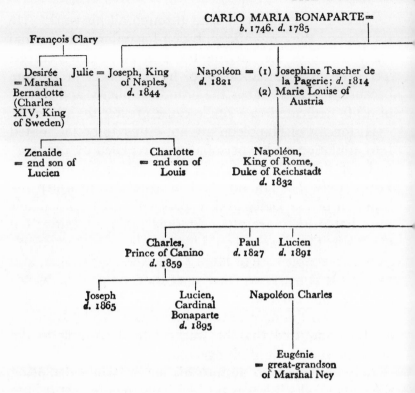

FAMILY

MARIE LETIZIA RAMOLINO
b. 1750. *d.* 1836

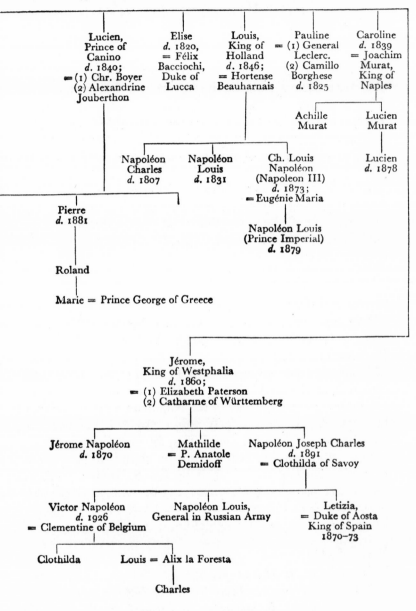

For Further Reading

Sources

Some of the most important sources for Napoleon's life have only become available in the last twenty-five years, notably: *Memoirs of Queen Hortense* (1927); *Memoirs of Caulaincourt, Duc de Vicence* (1933); *Letters of Napoleon to Marie-Louise* (1934); *General Bertrand's *Journal de St. Helène* (1948); *Memoirs of Marchand* (in course of publication); *Letters of Marie-Louise to Napoleon* ('My Dearest Louise' ed. C. F. Palmstierna 1958).

In addition to Napoleon's own *Correspondance* (1858–69) and *Memoirs* (1823), the more valuable memoirs of contemporaries include those of *Beugnot, *Chaptal, Fain, Marmont, *Meneval, *Metternich, Pasquier, Rapp, Roederer, Ségur, *Thibaudeau, *Thiébault. *Napoleon's Letters*, by J. M. Thompson (1934), provide a representative selection in translation.

Secondary Works

The best detailed biographies are those by: *A. Fournier (1891); *J. Holland Rose (1901); *F. Kircheisen (1931); *J. M. Thompson (1952).

Napoleon—For and Against, by P. Geyl (1949), is an interesting analysis of French historical literature on Napoleon.

The best general survey of the Napoleonic period, with a full bibliography, is the masterly volume by *G. Lefèbvre, *Napoléon* (Peuples et Civilisations Series, fourth edition, 1953).

Full bibliographies may also be found in L. Villat, *La Révolution et l'Empire*, vol. 2 (Clio Series, 1936); *G. Bruun, *Europe and the French Imperium* (1938), and J. Godechot *Les Institutions de la France sous la Révolution et l'Empire* (1951); F. Markham, *Napoleon* (Weidenfeld and Nicolson 1963).

Special Aspects

*O. Aubry, *St. Helena* (1937).
*H. Butterfield, *The Peace-Tactics of Napoleon* (1929).
G. Cavaignac, *Formation de la Prusse Contemporaine* (1897).
*D. Chandler, *The Campaigns of Napoleon* (1966).

178

A. Chuquet, *La Jeunesse de Napoléon* (1897).

J. Colin, *Éducation Militaire de Napoléon* (1900).

F. Crouzet, *L'Économie Britannique et le Blocus Continental* (1958).

*E. Dard, *Napoleon and Talleyrand* (1935).

*H. A. L. Fisher, *Napoleonic Statesmanship in Germany* (1903).

A. Fugier, *Napoléon et l'Espagne* (1930); *Napoléon et l'Italie* (1947).

P. Gonnard, *Origines de la Légende Napoléonienne* (1906).

*E. Hales, *Napoleon and the Pope* (1962).

M. Handelsman, *Napoléon et la Pologne* (1909).

*E. F. Hecksher, *The Continental System* (1922).

*J. Holland Rose, *Napoleonic Studies* (1904); *Personality of Napoleon* (1912).

H. Houssaye, *1814*; **1815*.

*W. C. Langsam, *Austrian Nationalism in the Napoleonic Wars* (1930).

A. Latreille, *L'Église et la Révolution*, vol. 2 (1950).

*J. Marshall-Cornwall, *Napoleon as Commander* (1967).

*A. Palmer, *Napoleon in Russia* (1967).

*Lord Rosebery, *Napoleon: The Last Phase* (1900).

P. Sagnac, *Législation Civile de la Révolution* (1898).

A. Sorel, *l'Europe et la Révolution Française* (1895–1909).

*Spenser Wilkinson, *The French Army before Napoléon* (1915); *The Rise of General Bonaparte* (1930).

*E. Tarlé, *Napoleon's Invasion of Russia* (1942).

J. Thiry, *Le Coup d'État de Brumaire* (1947).

A. Vandal, *L'Avènement de Bonaparte* (1903); *Napoléon et Alexandre I* (1896).

Note.—Books marked with an asterisk (*) are available in English.

Index

INDEX